Safeguarding Adults

Safeguarding Adults

Scamming and Mental Capacity

LEE-ANN FENGE, SALLY LEE and KEITH BROWN

$SAGE | **m** LearningMatters

Learning Matters
An imprint of SAGE Publications Ltd
1 Oliver's Yard
55 City Road
London EC1Y 1SP

SAGE Publications Inc.
2455 Teller Road
Thousand Oaks, California 91320

SAGE Publications India Pvt Ltd
B 1/I 1 Mohan Cooperative Industrial Area
Mathura Road
New Delhi 110 044

SAGE Publications Asia-Pacific Pte Ltd
3 Church Street
#10-04 Samsung Hub
Singapore 049483

Editor: Kate Keers
Production controller: Chris Marke
Project management: Swales and Willis Ltd, Exeter, Devon
Marketing manager: Camille Richmond
Cover design: Wendy Scott
Typeset by: C&M Digitals (P) Ltd, Chennai, India
Printed in the UK

Library of Congress Control Number: 2017935029

British Library Cataloguing in Publication Data

A catalogue record for this book is available from the British Library

ISBN 978-1-5264-2477-8
ISBN 978-1-5264-2478-5 (pbk)

Contents

About the editors

Dr Lee Ann-Fenge is Deputy Director of the National Centre for Post-Qualifying Social Work at Bournemouth University. She is a qualified social worker, and has worked in settings with both adults and children. Her research interests concern inclusive and creative research methodologies for engaging with seldom heard groups, practice with older people, financial scams and leadership. She teaches around the topics of adult safeguarding and leadership and supervision, has a numerous publications linked to her research interests.

Dr Sally Lee is Post-Doctoral Research Fellow at the National Centre for Post-Qualifying Social Work and Professional Practice at Bournemouth University. She completed her doctoral research in 2016 exploring social work practice, physical disability and sexual well-being. She brings to her academic role extensive social work practice experience built up during more than 25 years of working in diverse practice settings and services. Her research interests focus on often marginalised populations and at present she is investigating the experience of financial abuse and the detriment to individuals and society beyond financial loss.

Professor Keith Brown holds academic and professional qualifications in social work, nursing, teaching and management. He has worked in university and local authority education and training for over 25 years, and is currently Director of the National Centre for Post-Qualifying Social Work and Professional Practice and Director of the Institute of Health and Social Care Integration, at Bournemouth University. He received the Linda Ammon Memorial Prize in 2005, awarded to the individual making the greatest contribution to education and training in the UK. He sits on the Department of Health Adult Safeguarding Advisory Board, the Joint Department of Health and Ministry of Justice National Mental Capacity Leadership forum and the Home Office Joint Financial task force.

About the authors and contributors

Louise Baxter graduated with a law degree from Greenwich University in 2001. In 2002 she joined East Sussex Trading Standards as a Fair Trading Officer based in advice, winning the Diploma in Consumer Affairs prize in 2003. Louise was appointed Senior Manager within the Service in 2009 and became Chair of the Consumer Empowerment Alliance. She is also Chair of the Protection of Vulnerable Consumers regional group and the Trading Standards Institute's Lead Officer for education and advice.

Louise has undertaken pioneering work in identifying scam victims including starting the Scams Hub in 2011. She fights tirelessly to stop scam mail, her work featuring in many national newspapers and programs highlighting the devastating effect of scams and fraud. She is working with mail providers, financial institutions and local and central government to find an effective sustainable solution for victims.

Louise is active in her local community and is Vice Chair of the Governing Board at a pioneer Free School. Louise is a mum of two to Floss (6) and Bert (4).

Trish Burls is Principal Officer, Trading Standards in the Borough of Croydon.

Dr Elisabeth Carter is a Senior Lecturer in Criminology at the University of Roehampton, where she teaches criminology, policing, forensic linguistics and qualitative and quantitative research methods. She also takes on consultancy work in investigative interview training, language as evidence, and rapport-building and body language. Elisabeth's research centres on the points at which language and the law intersect, and currently examines the transferability of research into practice, deception in police interviews, language and power, and the interactional strategies used in scam communications.

Tim Day is a Senior Trading Standards Officer with Hertfordshire Trading Standards where he specialises in the investigation of doorstep crime and rogue trading. He is also the Chartered Trading Standards Institute's Lead Officer for Doorstep Crime, Scams and Consumer Vulnerability and is in the final year of a Professional Doctorate for Criminal Justice, at the University of Portsmouth's Institute of Criminal Justice Studies. The focus of the doctorate is rogue trading and the research explores police records in order to improve understanding of the phenomenon, and in particular, the victimology, the MO used by the perpetrators, and the enforcement response incidents receive.

Jodie Gordon has been part of the National Trading Standards Scams Team since January 2016 and currently leads their national initiative, Friends Against Scams.

Friends Against Scams won a Government Counter Fraud Award for Excellence in Fraud Awareness and has an ever growing number of 'Friends' who, together, are Taking a Stand Against Scams. Jodie and the Friends Against Scams Team are delighted by the success of the initiative so far and are looking forward to seeing it continue to grow and make a difference.

Mike Lyne is a Registered Social Worker and Registered Mental Nurse with over 25 years' experience in health and social care. He is Programme Leader for the Mental Capacity Act 2005 programme at Bournemouth University. His current interests are in capacity and mental health legislation, consent to treatment issues, end of life care and substituted decision-making in health and social care.

Andrew Mason trained as an economist and later took an MBA at London Business School. Following an early career in the motor industry, construction services and management consultancy, two redundancies in the 1980s led to the creation of his own consultancy businesses. Thirty years later, he is still doing some consultancy, but is now focused on chairing Telford and Wrekin's Safeguarding Children and Adults Boards and working as a director of a housing association. He was chair of Telford and Wrekin PCT until its abolition in 2013. He is a doting grandfather, keen walker, inadequate golfer and longstanding supporter of Manchester City FC.

Sean Olivier is the Safeguarding Coordinator for a London authority. He has been a qualified social worker for over 13 years and was awarded a Master's degree in Social Policy & Management from the University of Cape Town in 2009. Sean has research interests in financial abuse, care homes and joint working with the emergency services.

Rebekah Salmon joined the National Trading Standards Scams Team in October 2015 focusing on managing the Call Blocking pilot, which helped to protect consumers from scam and nuisance calls. Following a sabbatical in 2016 spent travelling around India, Rebekah has been instrumental in launching Friends Against Scams.

Frances Wilson graduated with a degree in Classical Studies from Royal Holloway, University of London before completing a Master's in Law at the University of Sheffield. She has worked for the National Trading Standards Scams Team since December 2015. Frances primarily focuses on partnership work with charities and investigative activities working to identify the criminals behind scams. Frances is currently leading on a new Call Blocking project, which aims to protect consumers living with dementia.

Foreword

Financial scams are a growing social blight causing profound detriment to the health and well-being of individuals and the wider economy. Although scams have been going on for as long as humans have interacted, it is only now with the pioneering work going on in enforcement agencies, local authorities, trading standards and the voluntary and financial sectors that the true range, reach and impact of personal fraud is being recognised. Advances in technology have increased the opportunities for scammers to reach beyond national boundaries, but 'old tech' fraud (relying on face to face encounters, mail or telephone contact) remains prevalent, often targeting the lonely, socially isolated and people in vulnerable circumstances who do not have the supportive networks which protect us.

This book comes at a time of rising public awareness and increasing media coverage of financial scamming and legitimate organisations which target often older vulnerable citizens for multiple and repeat donations, or selling of multiple unwanted products where the consumer lacks awareness that they have already donated or purchased the product. The book brings together a range of professional voices that speak with passion, offering their expertise and practice wisdom about the blight of scams. The work creates a comprehensive evidence base which demonstrates the significance of this topic to agencies which engage with the public, and the necessity for practitioners to develop skills in recognising and dealing with financial abuse from scams.

On behalf of the editorial team I would like to thank the contributors for their work. Their commitment to this project has enabled core and essential information about scams to be collated into one source text, each contributor's perspective offering different and valuable insights. But perhaps more importantly, I would like to thank the contributors for their enthusiasm for creating this book, and their commitment to it as an important contribution to the fight against scams and unscrupulous business and fundraising practices.

Professor Keith Brown, Director, National Centre for
Post-Qualifying Social Work and Professional Practice (NCPQSW),
Centre for Leadership, Impact and Management Bournemouth (CLiMB)

Introduction

Lee-Ann Fenge and Sally Lee

Aims of the book

The aim of this book is to provide practitioners, who work within the context of safeguarding adults, insights into the challenges posed by financial abuse and specifically financial scams. This book comes at a time when there is increasing awareness of the range, extent and impact of financial crime (ONS Crime Survey, 2016), and this in turn has an impact on the ways in which agencies need to work together to tackle the issue. A particular focus of this book is to consider the challenges of safeguarding adults who may be vulnerable or at particular risk of becoming involved in financial scams. Society is changing rapidly in ways which create exciting opportunities, but also significant challenges. In the UK an ageing population, alongside public policy which has been driven by an austerity agenda, has resulted in challenges to the sustainability of high quality health and social care services. The development of a global economy, supported by the growth of the internet, is transforming lives of people across the world. At the same time these opportunities provide the perfect environment for criminals to take advantage of existing and new technologies to find ways of targeting the most vulnerable in society and defraud them. Financial scams are not a new phenomenon, but changing methods of mass communication have supported a proliferation of mass marketing frauds and scams which are able to target specific population groups, such as older people or those who may live alone and be socially isolated.

Who is the book for?

This book has been written for practitioners who come from a range of agencies and who come in contact with adults who may be at risk of harm from financial abuse and scams. This includes:

- local authority social workers and trading standards staff
- police
- health services
- housing

- the voluntary sector

- private health and social care providers

- financial services.

It is important that all practitioners and agencies are aware of their duties to safeguard those at risk of financial abuse: the Care Act 2014 and statutory guidance 2016 bring financial abuse from scamming into focus as an adult safeguarding concern. It is important that this duty is just not focused on financial abuse which may occur within families or caring relationships, but also acknowledges the threats posed by mass marketing fraud and scams. Research indicates that policy and practice around financial abuse has been focused primarily on abuse from family or carers, rather than scammers (Redmond, 2016).

The Care Act 2014 and statutory guidance builds on safeguarding policy and brings financial abuse into focus. The act defines financial and material abuse in s42 (3):

'Abuse' includes financial abuse; and for that purpose 'financial abuse' includes:

(a) having money or other property stolen;

(b) being defrauded;

(c) being put under pressure in relation to money or other property; and

(d) having money or other property misused.

Developing understanding about the detrimental impact of scams on victims' health and well-being demonstrates that this is a public health concern and a significant threat to national health and economic well-being.

Approaches and structure of the book

Professionals working in public services are likely to be in contact with current, or potential, victims of financial crime and it is essential that they have the skills and knowledge to be effective in their work to protect and prevent further harm. This means practitioners need 'in-depth knowledge and understanding of mass marketing fraud (and other forms of scamming) including how perpetrators set up scams and sustain victims' involvement in them' (Oliver et al., 2015, p360).

This book aims to provide readers with a coherent and comprehensive discussion looking at adult safeguarding policy and practice, mental capacity and scamming. Existing knowledge about scams and the factors which lead people to become vulnerable are explored throughout the book. It is written from practitioner perspectives, for practitioners, and provides key learning points, case studies, reflective exercises and learning summaries to demonstrate knowledge in action. It aims to provide practitioners with an understanding of the legislative context of safeguarding adults practice and financial scams, and in particular legislation and practice in relation to the role of key agencies such as trading standards. To be effective, practitioners also require an understanding of the shifting social environment in which they work, such as the changing national demographic profiles and policy priorities which are subject to national and international events, and these issues are explored throughout the book.

The order of chapters is designed to lead readers from the broad social context of adult safeguarding, to specific consideration of the risks posed by financial scams, and discussion of specific factors which may increase vulnerability to scam involvement.

Chapter 1 opens the book by setting the context of safeguarding adults within a wider social policy context. This includes consideration of the impact of legislation such as the Care Act 2014, and the influence of the well-being agenda on safeguarding adults activity.

Chapter 2 explores the context of financial abuse and how financial scams fit within the wider context of safeguarding adults activity. This chapter explores the impact of financial scams and the detriment they pose both in terms of financial loss and negative impact on well-being.

In Chapter 3 the discussion of scams includes consideration of the range, scope and type of scams and the victim experience of being scammed, and specifically considers the role of trading standards in supporting scam victims. Chapters 4 and 5 consider specific factors which may increase vulnerability to scam involvement. In Chapter 4 the connection between loneliness, social isolation and the potential of scam involvement is explored. With rising numbers of people self-reporting feelings of loneliness and social isolation, it is essential that practitioners are alert to the diversity of risks to health and well-being such feelings can result in. Chapter 5 considers the connection between dementia and scams. This is an important area for practitioners to consider as the number of people living with dementia is growing, and this population is especially vulnerable to scams as their financial capability may be reduced as a consequence of cognitive deterioration.

Building on consideration of cognitive impairment and financial capacity raised in Chapter 5, Chapter 6 offers a discussion of the Mental Capacity Act 2005. In particular this includes consideration of capacity to make financial decisions, the roles of Power of Attorney and Court of Protection, and best interests assessments in mental capacity practice. In the final two chapters the work of trading standards and the National Trading Standards Scams Team are discussed in detail, and finally there is an in-depth account of the risks posed by doorstep crime.

A key message of this book is that partnership approaches are core to adult safeguarding practice. This is essential as it offers a way of bringing together the expertise of professionals from across a diverse range of professions who each bring different skills and insights into the safeguarding process. It demonstrates the value of such partnerships in the development of safeguarding knowledge and skills by drawing contributions from educators, trading standards staff, social work professionals and academics, each providing unique insights into scamming from their professional perspective.

This book emerges from ongoing research and campaign activity around financial scams undertaken at the National Centre for Post-Qualifying Social Work and Professional Practice at Bournemouth University, in collaboration with the National Scams Team and the Chartered Institute of Trading Standards. In partnership with these agencies we are committed to develop both professional and public under-standing of the risks posed by financial scams, and improve safeguarding practice to protect the most vulnerable members of society from financial scams. We hope that this book will support readers to develop in-depth understanding of the topic, and that in turn this will result in improved adult safeguarding practice.

Chapter 1
The new landscape of adult safeguarding

Sally Lee

CHAPTER OUTCOMES

As a result of completing this chapter you will:

- Understand a range of social influences and policy priorities which inform adult safeguarding policy and practice.

- Understand the changes to adult safeguarding policy and practice introduced through Making Safeguarding Personal and the Care Act 2014.

- Understand the role and responsibilities of Safeguarding Adults Boards.

- Understand the foundations of the later theme of financial abuse, specifically scams.

Introduction: social influences and policy priorities which inform adult safeguarding policy and practice

This chapter sets out to consider how global and national social changes influence adult safeguarding policy and why awareness of this is important for practitioners undertaking safeguarding activities. Adult safeguarding policy and practice has to be responsive to social change in order to meet the diverse range of needs and circumstances of people.

Adult safeguarding means:

> - *Protecting an adult's right to live in safety, free from abuse and neglect.*
> - *People and organisations working together to prevent and stop abuse or neglect.*
> - *Promoting well-being.*
> - *Having regard (where appropriate) to the adult's views, wishes, feelings and beliefs in deciding any action.*
> - *Recognising that adults sometimes have complex interpersonal relationships and may be ambivalent, unclear or unrealistic about their personal circumstances.*
>
> *(Adapted from DH, 2016a, 14.7)*

This description of adult safeguarding is responsive to significant social changes, examples of which include:

- Improved health interventions and living conditions resulting in demographic change. The UK has an ageing population and people with profound disabilities and complex health conditions are now able to live full and active lives (POPPI, 2015; Age UK, 2015; Alzheimer's Society, 2016). This change has led to a focus on prevention in UK social policy which promotes the maintenance of good health into later life. Prevention is seen as a way to broaden the reach of scarce resources, but is also based on the link between good health and personal well-being (Bacon *et al.*, 2010).

  Age, disability and complex health conditions do not automatically lead to increased risk of abuse or neglect or the need for care and support services; however, associated factors such as social isolation are linked to increased risk (these factors are discussed in later chapters).

- Global economic upheaval resulting from the financial crash of 2007/8, and subsequent austerity cuts to public spending introduced in the UK and elsewhere. Adult social care has been subject to severe funding constraints, for example 26 per cent fewer older people now receive care and support services than in 2010 (Humphries *et al.*, 2016).

- Implementation of the Human Rights Act 1998, the Mental Capacity Act 2005 and equality legislation including the Equality Act 2010. These acts, and further legislation, are underpinned by the commitment to the equal worth of people resulting from global human rights movements (for example Amnesty International), civil rights movements and decades of campaigns by marginalised groups (for example the disability movement which has been instrumental in raising awareness of the inequality experienced by disabled people). UK social policy must be compliant with the Human Rights Act 1998 and the principles of empowerment and informed consent are now embedded in social care policy, seen particularly in the emphasis on person-centred approaches.

- Growing international interest in human well-being as a measure of social progress to complement traditional GDP measures (Penny, 2015). Personal well-being is understood to both increase the quality of life for the individual and improve national health and economic outcomes (Thomas and Evans, 2010; Bacon *et al.*, 2010). The concept of well-being now underpins social care policy in the Care Act 2014, part 1, section 1: 'Promoting individual well-being'.

- High profile scandals about the quality and organisation of care and welfare services which have led to serious case reviews or public inquiries. For example the case of Stephen Hoskin (Flynn, 2007), and institutions including Winterbourne View (Flynn and Citarella, 2012) and Mid Staffordshire Hospital (Francis, 2013). Such cases have raised awareness of adult abuse making safeguarding a policy priority.

- Technological advances in communications, monitoring and assistive technology. These advances create new and positive opportunities for different methods of care delivery, monitoring and social interaction. However, technology also creates new opportunities for abuse, for example online romance scams.

ACTIVITY *1.1*

Consider your area of professional practice; have the above points influenced the outcomes of your organisation and how these are achieved?

For example, how does your organisation demonstrate compliance with the Human Rights Act 1998, and what difference has technology made to the way your service operates?

The points are examples of social changes; can you identify other changes which have affected your organisation?

Policy priorities

The changes mentioned above are examples of social trends which have profoundly influenced the social care policies which practitioners enact. Three interconnected core priorities have subsequently emerged and now dominate health and social care policy: *prevention, personalisation and integration* (Glasby *et al.*, 2015). Lyn Romeo, Chief Social Worker for Adults in England, states that personalisation and integration in particular require practitioners to extend their knowledge about changing social contexts so that they can more effectively promote enablement and protection (Romeo, 2015).

These three policy priorities are now explored as it is important for practitioners to understand the wider context of adult safeguarding.

Prevention and adult safeguarding

The Local Government Association states that health prevention interventions are most effective when there is:

- Significant investment in building community capacity.

- Support delivered directly to local communities taking on this role.

- Signposting, information and advice for individuals to be directed to these options.

- Patient activation – engaged in decision about their own/family care.

- A supportive approach to primary prevention – ensuring the rest of the system is empowered to make the required changes at a community and population level.

- Co-operation with employers, the third sector and the local health and social care market to ensure that people are connected to their community, feel valued and do not face isolation.

(LGA and Ernst and Young, 2015, p12)

These points clarify the role of local and national government in supporting and enabling the social environment in which health prevention strategies can make a positive impact. Practitioners are required to put prevention strategies into action so an understanding of the conditions which enable effective prevention is crucial. The prevention agenda is now embedded in social care policy in part 1, section 2, Care Act 2014. Statutory guidance (DH, 2016a, 2.4) does not offer a definition of prevention or preventative activities, but states that these can range from whole-population measures aimed at promoting health, to individual interventions aimed at improving skills, functioning or reducing the impact of caring responsibilities.

Understanding the common causal factors which link poor health and well-being and vulnerability to abuse or neglect (as well as common ways of enabling prevention) reinforces the value of inter-agency partnership work. For example, social isolation and loneliness are linked to poor health outcomes (Bacon *et al.*, 2010; Cacioppo *et al.*, 2014) as well as vulnerability to abuse and neglect (Age UK, 2015), whilst the ability to access good quality information is linked to improved health and well-being, empowerment and safeguarding (DH, 2016a, s2). The reduction of social isolation and the provision of information are important aspects of prevention work and require practitioners from different professional groups to work together.

Historically prevention has not been a priority in adult safeguarding policy (Brammer, 2014). The review of No Secrets (DH, 2009) placed a new emphasis on prevention and the empowerment of individuals to maintain their own safety (SCIE, 2011a). The earlier absence reflects the difficulty of proving that harm has been prevented which, in part, results from the secrecy associated with abuse and neglect (SCIE, 2011a). The Care Act 2014 brings prevention into the heart of social care policy (s2) and to adult safeguarding specifically:

It is better to take action before harm occurs.

(DH, 2016a, 14.13)

CSCI (2008) identified 'building blocks' necessary for the prevention of abuse or neglect which echo the points made by the LGA regarding health prevention:

- People being informed of their rights to be free from abuse and supported to exercise these rights, including access to advocacy.

- A well trained workforce operating in a culture of zero tolerance of abuse.

- Sound framework for confidentiality and information sharing across agencies.

- Good universal services, such as community safety services.

- Need and risk assessments to inform people's choices.

- Options for support to keep safe from abuse, tailored to people's individual needs.

- Services that prioritise both safeguarding and independence.

- Public awareness of the issues.

(Faulkner and Sweeney, 2011)

The prevention agenda required by the Care Act 2014, s2 develops these building blocks, identifying preventative interventions and joint approaches overseen by Safeguarding Adults Boards:

- Primary interventions: to prevent abuse occurring in the first instance. For example, Safer Community Partnerships, education and information to increase awareness of adult abuse and improve financial literacy.

- Secondary interventions to identify and respond directly to allegations of abuse.

- Tertiary interventions to remedy negative and harmful consequences of abuse and prevent future occurrences.

(SCIE, 2011a; DH, 2016a, s2)

Local authorities can 'raise the profile of every citizen's right to be free from abuse' (CSCI, 2008, p33) by targeting clear and easily accessible information to those covered by safeguarding procedures, and those not currently using services or paying for services themselves. Effective ways of preventing abuse or neglect include:

- Advocacy services which can enable adults at risk to express themselves in potentially or actually abusive situations.

- Education to raise awareness for individuals and groups to enable them to protect themselves from abuse.

- Raising awareness of adult abuse within the general population.

- Reducing social isolation through links with the community so there are more people who can be alert to the possibility of abuse as well as provide links to potential sources of support for adults at risk and family carers.

- Provision of clear, accessible and appropriate information available in diverse formats.

- Development of Community Safety Partnerships between local authorities and partner organisations including the police and the voluntary sector.

ACTIVITY 1.2

Think about the meaning of prevention. How is prevention undertaken in your profes-sional setting and how do you know if, and when, an intervention has been successful?

Personalisation and adult safeguarding

Personalisation dominates current social care policy and practice, including adult safe-guarding (Brammer, 2014). The Care Act 2014 extends the scope of personalisation and promotes it as a means to enable well-being. Its legislative authority is com-plex as there is no single act which defines or describes personalisation; instead it is discerned from diverse social care legislation including the NHSCC Act 1990 and sub-sequent direct payment acts (1996, 2000, 2001, 2009) (Brammer, 2014). This makes the definition and use fluid and broader in scope.

Think Local Act Personal (2016) offers the following definition in its 'jargon busting' website:

> *A way of thinking about care and support services that puts you at the centre of the process of working out what your needs are, choosing what support you need and having control over your life. It is about you as an individual, not about groups of people whose needs are assumed to be similar, or about the needs of organisations.*

Personalisation represents a departure from previous service-led approaches:

> *Personalisation means thinking about public services and social care in a different way – starting with the person and their individual circumstances rather than the service. It affects everyone in adult care and support.*

> (SCIE, 2012a, p1)

It is an approach that was promoted by the Independent Living Movement and dis-ability organisations as a means to enable equal inclusion, access and participation in mainstream life (Beresford, 2013). Personalisation has resonance with professional practice focused on human rights and a concern for equality.

However, the success of personalisation across different populations of service users is contested (Glasby *et al.*, 2015), and critics question whether the policy has been pur-posefully used to extend the marketisation of care to reduce costs (Beresford, 2013; Lymbery, 2013). Personalisation policy also assumes that people are willing and able to maximise control over their lives (or have the support of someone willing to act as their representative) (Furedi, 2011). It is important for practitioners to be aware of such criticism of personalisation policy, as this aids critical reflection and alerts practi-tioners to potentially disempowering applications of personalisation theory.

The term personalisation is often used in association, or even interchangeably (SCIE, 2012), with person-centred care which:

discovers and acts on what is important to a person. It is a process for continual listening and learning, focusing on what are important to someone now and in the future, and acting on this in alliance with their family and their friends.

(Thompson *et al.*, 2008, p27)

Think Local Act Personal defines person-centred care as:

An approach that puts the person receiving care and support at the centre of the way care is planned and delivered.

(Think Local Act Personal, 2016)

Making Safeguarding Personal (MSP) applies the principles of person-centred care to adult safeguarding. MSP is an ongoing sector-led initiative which brings together the principles of personalisation, person-centred care and safeguarding; it is the 'driving force in changing the landscape of adult safeguarding' (Romeo, 2015).

MSP seeks to achieve:

- A personalised approach that enables safeguarding to be done with, not to, people.

- Practice that focuses on achieving meaningful improvement to people's circumstances rather than just on 'investigation' and 'conclusion'.

- An approach that utilises social work skills rather than just 'putting people through a process'.

- An approach that enables practitioners, families, teams and Safeguarding Adults Boards to know what difference has been made.

(LGA and ADASS, 2014)

The MSP approach is person-led and outcome focused, aiming towards resolution and recovery from abuse and neglect (Cooper *et al.*, 2016). This approach is built on research which recognises that the outcomes wanted by victims of abuse and neglect are often modest, for example an apology and reassurance that the abuse and neglect will not reoccur, rather than the often disproportionate and bureaucratic safeguarding process (Brammer, 2014).

MSP has resulted in safeguarding conversations with the person concerned or their representative at all the stages of safeguarding interventions. A total of 97 per cent of English councils report that people are now asked at the outset about what outcomes they want, and 85 per cent of council systems have changed to enable the record-ing of this information (Cooper *et al.*, 2016) which provides a basis for measuring progress. However, lack of resources is cited by councils as a reason why full implemen-tation of MSP has not yet been achieved (Cooper *et al.*, 2016). MSP aids prevention by enabling people to manage their own safety more effectively through involving the individual in every stage of the safeguarding intervention. Practitioners 'work with adults who may be at risk, to help them recognise potentially abusive situations and understand how they can protect themselves' (SCIE, 2015b, p5). However, dilemmas arise when victims decline intervention or do not recognise their experience as abusive or neglectful or refuse safeguarding interventions. Person-centred approaches require that practitioners take time to establish the 'length and breadth of the issue' (Olivier *et al.*, 2015, p369); that is, to understand the meaning of the situation to the individual, their social connections and the psychological meaning of the abuse or neglect. For example in respect to scams the utility of involvement in a scam may be important to the victim, so their finding alternative sources of meaning, purpose and social capital are crucial (Olivier *et al.*, 2015). Practitioners' ability to build trusting relationships with victims of abuse or neglect is crucial to making positive changes (SCIE, 2011a).

ACTIVITY **1.3**

In your experience, what do personalisation and person-centred care mean? How are personalisation and person-centred approaches promoted in your professional setting?

Integration and adult safeguarding

The UK Government aims for all local health and care services to be integrated by 2020 (HM Government, Autumn Statement, 2015).

In 2016 the LGA, NHS Confederation, the Association of Directors of Adult Social Services and NHS Clinical Commissioners jointly published *Stepping Up to the Place: The Key to Successful Health and Care Integration* which calls for the:

> *radical transformation of services in order to meet the needs of a society with increasingly chronic and complex health needs. The vision paves the way for integration and transformation to happen faster and to go further so that integrated and person-centred care becomes the mainstream.*

> (LGA, 2016a)

The cost savings associated with integration has meant that the policy has gained urgency in an environment of budget cuts where achieving more for less has become an accepted policy goal (Humphries *et al.*, 2016). This requires:

> *achieving better outcomes within existing resources ... better management of demand, promoting independence, better commissioning and procurement and implementing models of integrated care that give best outcomes, rather than shunting costs between each other.*

> (LGA, 2016b)

Integration aims to aid adult safeguarding by reducing the risk of abuse and neglect through improving:

- personalised care which considers the individual's 'broader life journey' rather than treatment alone;

- opportunities of independence;

- mortality rates;

- inter-service communication;

- appropriate hospital admissions;

- personal and community well-being;

- community networks.

(LGA and Ernst and Young, 2015, p16)

Safeguarding adults and the Care Act 2014

The Care Act 2014 is a major piece of reforming legislation consolidating many of the multiple laws relating to social care. The act makes adult safeguarding a statutory responsibility for the first time. Prior to the implementation of the Care Act 2014, adult safeguarding policy and practice was based on guidance provided by *No Secrets* (DH, 2000).

No Secrets was an acknowledgement of adult abuse in the light of growing recognition and understanding about the frequency and types of abused adults' experience, and promoted the notion that, 'There can be no secrets and no hiding places when it comes to exposing the abuse of vulnerable adults' (DH, 2000, Foreword).

Human rights discourse was used throughout *No Secrets* (Brammer, 2014), including directly linking the definition of abuse with a contravention of rights:

Abuse is a violation of an individual's human and civil rights by any other person or persons.

(DH, 2000, 2.3)

No Secrets and the subsequent National Framework for Safeguarding Adults (2005) built on themes of partnership, prevention and service user and carer consultation, which have been further developed by the Care Act and can be seen in the new duties given to local authorities.

Care Act safeguarding duties

The duties are set out in sections 42–46 of the act and Chapter 14 of the statutory guidance. A local authority must:

- make enquiries, or ensure others do so, if it believes an adult is, or is at risk of, abuse or neglect. An enquiry should establish whether any action needs to be taken to stop or prevent abuse or neglect, and if so, by whom;

- set up a Safeguarding Adults Board (SAB);

- arrange, where appropriate, for an independent advocate to represent and support an adult who is the subject of a safeguarding enquiry or Safeguarding Adult Review, where the adult has 'substantial difficulty' in being involved in the process, and where there is no other appropriate adult to help them;

- cooperate with each of its relevant partners in order to protect adults experiencing or at risk of abuse or neglect.

(DH, 2016a, 14.10)

Eligibility for section 42 enquiries

There are no eligibility criteria for section 42 adult safeguarding enquiries; instead this is dependent on the individual's ability to protect themselves due to any care and support needs. Adult safeguarding duties apply to any adult who:

- has care and support needs (whether or not the local authority is meeting any of those needs); and

- is experiencing, or is at risk of, abuse or neglect; and

- is unable to protect themselves because of their care and support needs.

(s42 (1))

Local authorities also have 'safeguarding responsibilities for carers and a general duty to promote the well-being of the wider population in the communities they serve' (SCIE, 2015b, p2). The enquiry may be informal, such as a conversation with the individual, or formal involving multi-agency action planning.

An enquiry seeks to:

- establish the facts;

- ascertain the adult's views and wishes;

- assess the needs of the adult for protection, support and redress and how they might be met;

- protect from the abuse and neglect, in accordance with the wishes of the adult;

- make decisions as to what follow-up action should be taken with regard to the person or organisation responsible for the abuse or neglect;

- enable the adult to achieve resolution and recovery.

(Galpin, 2016, p38)

The principles of person-centred care are evident in the enquiry objectives aligning safeguarding with personalised ways of working, drawing on the principles of Making Safeguarding Personal and personalisation.

Key principles underpinning adult safeguarding

> ## *When the principles are effectively used an individual would be able to agree with the following statements:*
>
> *People worked together to reduce risk to my safety and well-being.*
>
> *I had the information I needed; in the way that I needed it.*
>
> *Professionals helped me to plan ahead and manage the risks that were important to me.*
>
> *People and services understood me – recognised and respected what I could do and what I needed help with.*
>
> *The people I wanted were involved.*
>
> *I had good quality care – I felt safe and in control.*
>
> *When things started to go wrong, people around me noticed and acted early.*
>
> *People worked together and helped when I was harmed.*
>
> *People noticed and acted.*
>
> *People asked what I wanted to happen and worked together with me to get it.*
>
> *I got the help I needed by those in the best place to give it.*
>
> *The help I received made my situation better.*
>
> *People will learn from my experience and use it to help others.*
>
> *I understood the reasons when decisions were made that I didn't agree with.*
>
> *(DH, 2013, 5.3)*

Empowerment

The ideals of personalisation and person-centred approaches are founded on empowerment which the Care Act 2014 promotes through the 'presumption of person-led decisions and informed consent' (The College of Social Work, 2014, p1).

People need to be able to say: 'I am asked what I want as the outcomes from the safeguarding process and these directly inform what happens' (DH, 2013, 5.2; DH, 2016a, 14.13).

Organisations need to be able to say: 'We give individuals the right information about how to recognise abuse and what they can do to keep themselves safe. We give them clear and simple information about how to report abuse and crime and what support we can give. We consult them before we take any action. Where someone lacks capacity to make a decision, we always act in his or her best interests' (DH, 2013, 5.4).

Empowerment is rooted in human rights, and the Human Rights Act (HRC) 1998 sets out the fundamental rights and freedoms that everyone in the UK is entitled to. People have a right to live free from abuse (Galpin, 2016) and it is the duty of statutory agencies to protect this right. Failure to protect, resulting in serious abuse (including financial abuse), can constitute a violation of Article 3, HRC 1998. However, protection has to be balanced with other human rights such as the right to respect of family and private life (Article 8) which states that public authorities cannot control who an individual corresponds with or forges relationships with (including scammers) except in exceptional circumstances or where mental capacity is an issue. In addition Protocol 1, Article 1 protects citizens' right to enjoy their property, such as their financial assets, which means that a public authority cannot remove property or place restrictions on its use, unless there is good reason to do so, such as coercion or mental capacity concerns. This illustrates the balance public agencies need to achieve between the right to protection and the right to privacy (Article 8). Balancing these requirements creates dilemmas for professionals and carers working with people at risk of abuse and neglect.

Prevention

It is better to take action before harm occurs.

I receive clear and simple information about what abuse is, how to recognise the signs and what I can do to seek help.

(DH, 2013, 5.2; DH, 2016a, 14.13)

Organisations need to be able to say: 'We help the community to identify and report signs of abuse and suspected criminal offences. We train staff how to recognise signs and take action to prevent abuse occurring. In all our work, we consider how to make communities safer' (DH, 2013, 5.4).

Prevention has become a policy priority in part because of financial necessity, but also due to growing interest in human well-being. The Care Act 2014 introduces the well-being principle requiring local authorities to ensure that all functions, activities and outcomes are mindful of, and aim to enhance, well-being (s1). The act also redefines eligibility for social care interventions in terms of 'risk to well-being' as opposed to the 'risk to independence' as previously set out in Fair Access to Care (DH 2003, updated in 2010). The link between the impact on well-being of abuse and neglect puts safeguarding at the core of all local authority work and reinforces that 'safeguarding is everybody's business' (DH, 2013).

Proportionality

Individuals need to be able to say: 'I am sure that the professionals will work in my interest, as I see them and they will only get involved as much as needed' (DH, 2013, 5.2; DH, 2016a, 14.13).

Organisations need to be able to say: 'We discuss with the individual and where appropriate, with partner agencies what to do where there is risk of significant harm before we take a decision' (DH, 2013, 5.4).

Risk is an element of many situations and should be part of any wider assessment.

Proportionality is relevant to all Care Act assessment activities (DH, 2016a, 6.3) and concerns balancing the risk in the least intrusive way in order to achieve an objective (Brammer, 2014).

Protection

Individuals need to be able to say: 'I get help and support to report abuse and neglect. I get help so that I am able to take part in the safeguarding process to the extent to which I want' (DH, 2013, 5.2; DH, 2016a, 14.13).

Organisations need to be able to say: 'We have effective ways of assessing and managing risk. Our local complaints and reporting arrangements for abuse and suspected criminal offences work well. Local people understand how we work and how to contact us. We take responsibility for putting them in touch with the right person' (DH, 2013, 5.4).

The need to protect has to be balanced with the promotion of autonomy and assessment capacity is crucial to negotiating risk and protection. This is discussed further in Chapter 6.

Partnership

People need to be able to say: 'I know that staff treat any personal and sensitive information in confidence, only sharing what is helpful and necessary. I am confident that professionals will work together and with me to get the best result for me' (DH, 2013, 5.2; DH, 2016a, 14.13).

Organisations need to be able to say: 'We are good at sharing information locally. We have multi-agency partnership arrangements in place and staff understand how to use these. We foster a "one" team approach that places the welfare of individuals before the "needs" of the system' (DH, 2013, 5.4).

The Care Act 2014 maintains the local authority as the lead partner in adult safeguarding (apart from cases led by police), but strengthens the obligation of partnership work (DH, 2016a, 14.62–14.67). SCIE (2015) emphasises the importance of partnership approaches to adult safeguarding.

Accountability

People need to be able to say: 'I understand the role of everyone involved in my life and so do they' (DH, 2013, 5.2; DH, 2016a, 14.13).

Organisations need to be able to say: 'The roles of all agencies are clear, together with the lines of accountability. Staff understand what is expected of them and others. Agencies recognise their responsibilities to each other, act upon them and accept collective responsibility for safeguarding arrangements' (DH, 2013, 5.4).

Accountability can be linked to the promotion of human rights within social policy, and aids the protection of people from the misuse of power, abuse or neglect by public authorities. Other services are accountable to bodies such as the Care Quality Commission, a non-departmental public body of the Department of Health, which is responsible for the registration and inspection of health and social care providers. Professionals are personally accountable for their work and conduct, linked to codes of conduct, terms of employment and the registration of some health and social care professionals, and complaints procedures reinforce accountability.

Roles and responsibilities of Safeguarding Adults Boards (SAB)

Partnership and integrated working is at the heart of current social policy. Strategic direction and oversight is required to develop effective organisational partnerships and create a shared agenda to protect adults at risk of abuse or neglect. Serious case reviews have frequently highlighted the absence of inter-agency communication and collaboration (Brammer, 2014). This is the core task for SABs, which have been made a statutory requirement by the Care Act 2014. Each board must assure itself that the local safeguarding policy and practice of all partners acts to help protect adults in the area who meet section 42 criteria (Galpin, 2016).

This assurance is dependent on local safeguarding arrangements and practice:

- meeting the requirements of the Care Act 2014 and statutory guidance;
- being person-centred and outcome-focused;
- working collaboratively to prevent abuse and neglect where possible;
- ensuring agencies and individuals give timely and proportionate responses when abuse or neglect have occurred;
- continuously improving and enhancing the quality of life of adults in its area.

(SCIE, 2016)

The SAB provides strategic oversight for the locality, working with a wide breadth of services and organisations to prevent abuse and neglect, including NHS, education, police, trading standards and the independent care sector. SABs are required to create an open culture around safeguarding, where partners can challenge each other, when appropriate, and advice and guidance can be sought (SCIE, 2016, p8).

The SAB has three core duties:

- To develop and publish a strategic plan, setting out how they will meet their objectives and how their member and partner agencies will contribute.

- To publish an annual report detailing how effective their work has been.

- To commission safeguarding adults reviews (SARs) for any cases which meet the criteria for these.

(SCIE, 2016)

CASE STUDY **1.1**

Telford and Wrekin Safeguarding Adults Board (SAB) was established in 2015 directly as a result of the Care Act. Telford partners recognised that the Act provided the basis for a more locally based approach to safeguarding adults than had been possible with a joint board with Shropshire.

At first, we focused on making the new Board compliant with the Care Act through defining new governance arrangements and structures and adopting the established West Midlands regional safeguarding procedures. The development of an effective partnership was made easier by my having chaired the Safeguarding Children Board since 2012, with many Children's Board members agreeing to serve on the new Board. From the start, we explored how both Boards could work better together and have recently supported the creation of an 'all family' MASH and are now making Children's Domestic Abuse a priority sub-group of both Boards. We are also planning a cross-board communications campaign around the theme of discouraging people from being bystanders when they observe abuse and neglect in the community.

In working together, it became clear that there was some confusion regarding the strategic responsibilities of other partnership Boards, the Health and Wellbeing Board, the Community Safety Partnership and the Early Help Partnership, particularly with respect to emerging issues such as female genital mutilation, modern slavery and forced marriage. We therefore encouraged a debate across the partnership on how we could work better together. This has resulted in the creation of an integrated Partnership Management function within the local authority which supports all five Boards and facilitates a coordinated response to strategy development, priority setting and the allocation of responsibilities.

Making Safeguarding Personal (MSP) has been a major challenge. While some progress has been made in re-engineering processes in adult social care so that MSP is an integral part of service delivery, this approach is not yet fully embedded across the partnership. We are therefore developing a capability framework to clearly set our expectations for staff

(Continued)

competency, particularly in relation to MSP. This framework will be implemented across partners' agencies represented on the Board via a multi-agency learning and development plan, which will support delivery of the framework and ensure staff are competent and capable. The approach to delivering the framework will focus less on formal guidance and training, but more on action learning sets which involve themed events for partners and relevant staff focusing on key issues/areas for development highlighted as part of implementation of the framework.

We have also experienced difficulties in improving engagement with the local community and have had a number of false starts, fruitless debates, duplication of existing initiatives and unsuccessful public events, where we have struggled to put over a simple message to audiences with little interest in the subject matter.

We do however feel we may have found the solution in piloting the concept of 'Conversation Cafés' at local care homes, where we have established a network of individuals who are willing to regularly engage with the Board on specific questions in relation to the work of the Board, its plans and priorities through an informal drop-in session. We are now developing a generic leaflet introducing the Board and its Conversation Café approach for Board members to hand out to groups and individuals who they feel may want to contribute now or in the future.

At our last Board it was agreed that having established a compliant Board we should become more ambitious in how we try to improve the safety and security of adults in our community. All Board members have submitted ideas for a Board Development day and one suggestion, resulting from the Chair's attendance at a CEnTSA conference on Financial Abuse, is that this issue should form the basis for the Board's first priority sub-group.

Andrew Mason, Independent Chair
Telford and Wrekin Safeguarding Adults Board

The case study illustrates how collaboration is key to the work of SABs, as set out in the co-operation duties of the Care Act 2014 to:

- increase knowledge about prevalence and types of abuse and neglect, and when referral for enquiry is necessary through analysis of local data;

- develop preventative approaches;

- ensure safeguarding practice is person-centred and outcome-focused;

- ensure agencies and individuals are accountable and give timely and proportionate responses when abuse or neglect have occurred;

- ensure safeguarding practice is continuously improving and enhancing the quality of life of adults in its area;

- balance the requirements of confidentiality with the consideration that, to protect adults, it may be necessary to share information on a 'need-to-know basis' (s45);

- develop multi-agency training and consider any specialist training that may be required.

(Adapted from DH, 2016a, 14.139)

Key learning points

- Adult social care policy emerges from a social context informed by national and global events and movements.

- Safeguarding policy and practice is influenced by person-centred approaches to care and support.

- These approaches emphasise the empowerment of individuals to be active agents and decision-makers whilst being supported to manage risk.

- Abuse of any kind undermines health and well-being.

- The Care Act 2014 provides the statutory foundation for adult safeguarding policy and practice.

- The Act introduces new safeguarding duties.

- Safeguarding Adults Boards are a mandatory requirement. They are responsible for developing partnership approaches to keeping their communities safe.

- The Care Act 2014 introduces the well-being principle which all care and support functions and activities must promote.

Chapter 2

Adult safeguarding and financial abuse from scams

Sally Lee, with contribution from Louise Baxter

CHAPTER OUTCOMES

As a result of completing this chapter you will:

- Understand what constitutes financial abuse from scams and how to recognise it.

- Understand how financial abuse from scams impacts on individuals, their networks and wider society.

- Understand s42 duties in relation to financial abuse from scams.

- Understand the broader responsibilities professionals have regarding scamming.

Introduction

Financial abuse is the second most common form of abuse (Adult Social Care Statistics, 2016). There is a substantial body of research evidence concerning financial abuse perpetrated by abusers known personally to the victim (for example: SCIE, 2011; Gibson and Qualls, 2012; Redmond, 2016). Less is understood about financial abuse in the form of scamming. Redmond (2016) suggests that it is understandable that attention has been on the

> common perpetrators of abuse and contexts where it takes place [but this] has meant that those working in the field of adult safeguarding have not been focused on those activities that take place on the margins and with events and practices that take place in plain sight and 'under our own noses'.

> (Redmond, 2016, p90)

Redmond identifies unscrupulous charitable and religious fundraising as the kind of financially abusive behaviours which occur 'on the margins', taking place 'under our noses'. This chapter extends the scope of these abusive behaviours to include the fraud perpetrated by scammers, who use the same marketing techniques and psychological insights into consumer behaviour as legitimate business to extract assets from people made vulnerable by their circumstances.

Financial abuse

The word abuse is used to denote a broad range of actions committed with the intent to harm, or acts of omission where due diligence has been neglected. Its meaning includes notions of exploitation for personal gain, which might relate to the expression of power, sexual gratification or financial advantage (Brammer, 2014).

Davidson *et al.* (2015) found that the definition of financial abuse of older people most frequently cited in research and literature is:

> *The illegal or improper exploitation or use of funds or other resources of the older person.*
>
> (WHO, 2008, cited in Davidson *et al.*, 2015, p3)

However, financial abuse is more ambiguous than the definition suggests, due to issues of victim consent and social expectation. For example, family members have suggested that because they expect to inherit their relative's assets after their death, accessing it prematurely cannot be considered theft (SCIE, 2011a). This ambiguity has led to the term 'financial abuse' being criticised for both downplaying the seriousness of this form of exploitation and, conversely, for being 'unnecessarily stigmatising and inflammatory' (Brown, 2003, p4).

The Care Act 2014 and statutory guidance builds on safeguarding policy and brings financial abuse into focus. The act defines financial and material abuse in s42 (3):

> *'Abuse' includes financial abuse; and for that purpose 'financial abuse' includes:*
>
> *(a) having money or other property stolen;*
>
> *(b) being defrauded;*
>
> *(c) being put under pressure in relation to money or other property; and*
>
> *(d) having money or other property misused.*

The statutory guidance (2016) states:

> *Financial or material abuse include[es] theft, fraud, internet scamming, coercion in relation to an adult's financial affairs or arrangements, including in connection with wills, property, inheritance or financial transactions, or the misuse or misappropriation of property, possessions or benefits.*
>
> (DH, 2016a, 14.17)

This statement clearly links the experience of being scammed with local authority safeguarding responsibilities. The statement is broad in its approach which does not limit who an abuser might be (stranger or family/carer), nor does it specify the nature of the relationship between victim and abuser, nor the particular methods of abuse.

REFLECTION 2.1

Write down a definition of financial abuse in one sentence.

Think about the intention of the 'abuser'; what influence does this have on your definition?

Do you think an action can be termed financial abuse if the individual consents? Are there degrees of consent?

Do you think financial abuse shares any characteristics with other forms of abuse, for example physical intimidation?

Scamming is a particular form of financial abuse perpetrated by unscrupulous traders or criminals who employ legitimate marketing techniques to sell non-existent, valueless or poor quality goods, or engage consumers in bogus schemes such as investment fraud. Types of scams are discussed in Chapters 3 and 8.

Legislation protects all consumers from scams which the Fraud Act 2006 defines as fraudulent criminal activity committed in three specific ways with different scams falling into each category:

(a) Fraud by false representation.

(b) Fraud by failing to disclose information.

(c) Fraud by abuse of position.

(Fraud Act 2006, chapter 35 (1))

The Consumer Protection from Unfair Trading Regulations 2008 adds to this definition by making misleading actions or omissions by traders a criminal offence. This includes unscrupulous behaviour by legitimate traders such as deceit or hiding/omitting crucial information leading the person to enter into a transaction they would not normally do or would not do if they had the full information (Age UK, 2015). Schedule 1 of the Regulations sets out specific banned practices relevant to scams such as creating the false impression that the consumer has already won a prize, or will win, or will on doing a particular act when there is no prize and results in 'persistent unwanted solicitation by phone or email and pretending that a prize has been won' (schedule 1, 2008).

Research indicates that scamming is an enormous problem. The Crime Survey, England and Wales states that from October 2015 to September 2016: 'Experimental Statistics showed there were 3.6 million fraud and 2.0 million computer misuse offences for the first full year in which such questions have been included in the CSEW' (Office for National Statistics, 2017, p1). Scams cross international borders, made easier by the growing reach of the internet, making it a global concern.

Scams can be a one-off event or a longer-term interaction resulting in chronic victimisation (SCIE, 2011a).

REFLECTION 2.2

Make a list of all the financial scams you can think of.

Who do you think each scam might be targeted at?

Why do you think those particular people would be targeted?

When is an s42 adult safeguarding enquiry appropriate in cases of scamming?

Victims of scams may require safeguarding interventions. The safeguarding duties apply to an adult who:

- has needs for care and support (whether or not the local authority is meeting any of those needs);

- is experiencing, or at risk of, abuse or neglect;

- as a result of those care and support needs is unable to protect themselves from either the risk of, or the experience of abuse or neglect.

(s42 (1))

The question of whether the individual is able to protect themselves is at the core of the criterion for s42 enquiries, hence the need for a capacity assessment at the outset of safeguarding work. This includes considering:

- ways of managing risk for those who have capacity yet wish to continue the abusive relationship/activity; and

- whether they are being coerced/subject to undue influence which may lead to looking at inherent jurisdiction decisions.

(DH, 2016a)

Local authorities have discretion to conduct s42 enquiries 'for people where there is not a section 42 duty, if the local authority believes it is proportionate to do so, and will enable the local authority to promote the person's well-being and support a preventative agenda' (14.44 Care Act Guidance).The sharing of multi-agency expertise is key to such situations with, amongst other agencies, adult social care, housing, trading standards, the police and the financial sector each bringing particular expertise.

For example, trading standards bring expertise on consumer protection to safe-guarding which other agencies may not have. As discussed in Chapter 1, enabling partnership working to enhance the prevention of abuse and neglect is a core responsibility of the Safeguarding Adults Boards and the introduction of Multi-Agency Safeguarding Hubs (MASH) is a demonstration of this partnership in practice.

CASE STUDY **2.1**

Mr and Mrs J are both in their 80s. They were previously unknown to adult social care, trading standards or the police.

Trading standards received an alert from the National Scams Team as a cheque from Mr J was found in seized scam mail concerning a bogus investment company. A local trading standards officer contacted Mr J to arrange a home visit. Mr J was initially reluctant to agree to a visit; however, on being informed that a large amount of mail had been seized he agreed to meet.

During the visit the officer observed that the property was cold and in need of basic maintenance. The environment was cluttered with boxes and what appeared to be large amounts of post. Mrs J was present during the visit, but remained withdrawn. It was apparent that she required assistance with mobilising and the officer suspected that her personal hygiene was poor.

Mr J stated that he had always controlled their financial affairs and had up-to-date knowledge about appropriate investments. The trading standards officer provided information about investment scams and how Mr J's name had come to the attention of the scams team. Mr J admitted that he had invested a considerable amount of money in diamonds over the preceding 5 years. He stated that he was confident that he would be getting a good return on his investment. Mr J denied that his investments were scams despite being presented with contradictory evidence. The officer provided information about potential financial help with household repairs, benefits and services from adult social care including a carer's assessment. Mr J admitted that he was struggling to help Mrs J because her health had recently deteriorated. Both Mr and Mrs J agreed to a further visit and a referral to adult social care.

A referral was made to the local safeguarding team as the trading standards officer had reasonable grounds for believing Mrs J was at risk of abuse and neglect and was unable to protect herself due to her health conditions. A joint visit with trading standards and adult social care was subsequently arranged.

During the visit the social worker spoke to Mrs J privately to ascertain both her views and mental capacity. Mrs J disclosed that she was extremely concerned about her husband's behaviour as he had become increasingly secretive and aggressive when she requested anything which had a financial cost, for example putting on the central heating. She confirmed that he controlled their finances, but she had always felt confident in his ability to do so until 2 years ago when she became aware that maintenance jobs around their home were being neglected. When she asked him about this he became angry and said they could not afford to do any work on the property, despite his pension and their savings. She was also aware of the increased amount of post. His behaviour had caused arguments with their children who

---

he had subsequently stopped from making contacting with her. She stated that although she did not think he would deliberately hurt her, she did not believe he could provide the help she needed because of his own ill-health. Mrs J declined respite care stating that she did not want to leave her home. The social worker gained consent to contact Mrs J's family. Concerns about Mrs J's safety were shared with her, but she stated that she wished to have her care needs met at home. Medical evidence revealed that Mrs J had been diagnosed with rheumatoid arthritis 15 years ago, but there was no evidence of cognitive impairment.

The social worker completed an assessment with Mrs J and identified that support was needed with washing and dressing, along with referrals to the continence advisory service, Citizens Advice for support with claiming additional benefits such as Attendance Allowance, the fire service for fire safety advice and the falls prevention service.

The social worker undertook a carer's assessment with Mr J who had disclosed his financial concerns to the trading standards officer, revealing that he had spent the couple's life savings on investments which he now realised were bogus. He also admitted to buying goods from catalogues to be entered into prize draws. He stated that the amount of post he was now receiving was overwhelming and causing him anxiety. He expressed anger at the scammers but also at himself. He admitted that he had refused to allow his family to arrange any support for Mrs J and this had caused a family rift. He felt humiliated and did not want to admit to their children that the money had been spent.

Outcome: *Mrs J received the care and support services she needed in the place she wanted. The financial assessment revealed that their substantial savings had been depleted to the extent that state funded care was necessary. A charitable organisation assisted with property maintenance and ensuring all relevant benefits had been claimed. Mr and Mrs J's family re-established contact which has helped Mrs J regain her self-confidence.*

Trading standards supported Mr J to cease all correspondence with catalogues, prize draws and lotteries and provided advice and education about investment scams helping him realise that he was not the only person taken in by the scam. Mr J was encouraged to help gather evidence to enable enforcement and prosecution. He became a Mail Marshal (see Chapter 7) thereby helping other victims. These activities helped him regain a sense of pride.

Mr and Mrs J agreed to the installation of a telephone blocker and the postal preference service helping them regain control of who contacts them.

Trading standards, adult social care and other agencies worked together to enable Mr and Mrs J to become scam-aware and protect themselves.

Recognising financial abuse and working with victims of scams

The secrecy associated with financial and material abuse and the diversity of presentations, forms and experiences of those who have been financially abused add to the difficulty in recognising and addressing it (Samsi *et al.*, 2014; Redmond, 2016).

The choice agenda promoted within social policy, particularly through personalisation, along with legislation including the Mental Capacity Act 2005 and the Care Act 2014 promote people's right to make choices, including unwise choices (principle 3, MCA 2005). Practitioners from all agencies are required to work in person-centred ways, promoting autonomy. This creates practice dilemmas in situations where people have chosen to participate in scams, sometimes even after they have been informed that the transaction is abusive, exploitative, and might even be funding criminal activity. Assessment of capacity is crucial and guides further intervention, with the Court of Protection and Lasting Power of Attorney offering protective options for those assessed as lacking capacity to manage their financial affairs (discussed in Chapter 6; dementia is discussed in Chapter 5). Financial abuse is more likely to occur in settings where there is little external scrutiny (O'Keefe *et al.*, 2007, cited in Brammer, 2014), which further obscures the extent and range of this type of abuse. In addition the reluctance of some victims to disclose their experiences perhaps because of fear of reprisal, or even recognise their experience as abusive, means that the information recorded about incidents of financial abuse does not reflect the true situation (Gibson and Qualls, 2012; Age UK, 2015).

Protecting individuals assessed as having capacity to manage their financial affairs, yet who refuse to protect themselves by altering their behaviour, is more complex. The courts recognise that 'between active decision-makers and those certified as lacking mental capacity is a category of vulnerable adults who are open to exploitation' (Sofaer, 2012) (refer to *DL v A Local Authority and Others* [2012] EWCA Civ 253 for case law illustrating how the Court of Appeal decided that statutes and precedents cannot be applied in ways which leave the vulnerable at risk (Lee *et al.*, in press)). Scammers can exert undue influence on their victims, effectively grooming them, resulting in the individual's judgement being compromised. In cases of suspected coercion, when the Mental Capacity Act 2005 is not applicable, a local authority can apply to the courts 'to exercise its inherent jurisdiction to protect an adult with mental capacity' (SCIE, 2014). Such action aims to ensure that the individual's decisions are made freely rather than override their choices, no matter how 'unwise' they might be (Lee *et al.*, in press).

Links can be made between aspects of self-neglect (identified by the Care Act 2014 as a form of abuse and neglect (RiPfA, 2016)), and individuals who maintain their involvement in scams: these are individuals who act against their own best interests, often depriving themselves of basic care or provisions.

Quote from scam victim provided by Louise Baxter, National Trading Standards Scams Team

I have neglected myself in that I have gone without food, or fuel to heat my home, just to ensure that I had enough money in my cheque book to send money off to these letters. At no point did I ever think that these were scam letters and that there was no prize coming my way.

In such cases, 'It is essential to try to "find the person" by learning what you can about their life history and social, economic, psychological and physical situation'

(RiPfA, 2016, p3). This is described by Olivier *et al.* (2015, p369) as taking time to establish the 'length and breadth of the issue'. This includes: understanding the utility and meaning of the scam to the individual; the length of scam involvement; key life events affecting the individual during this period; their social connections; and the psychological meaning of the scam for them.

Evidence-informed strategies for working with people who self-neglect can be used when engaging with scam victims who choose to continue their involvement. This means aiming to:

- build rapport and trust — showing respect, empathy, persistence and continuity;
- seek to understand the meaning and significance of the self-neglect, taking account of the individual's life experience;
- work patiently at the pace of the individual, and knowing when to make the most of moments of motivation to secure change;
- constantly review the individual's mental capacity to make self-care decisions;
- communicate about risks and options with honesty and openness, particularly where coercive action is a possibility;
- ensure options for intervention are rooted in sound understanding of legal powers and duties;
- think flexibly about how family members and community resources can contribute to interventions, building on relationships and networks;
- proactively engage and coordinate agencies with specialist expertise to contribute towards shared goals.

(RiPfa, 2016, p2)

These strategies reflect the most effective ways of engaging with scam victims identified by the National Trading Standards Scams Team (2015).

Such longer-term, relationship-based approaches to practice may be more difficult to maintain or justify due to austerity cuts to local authority services; nonetheless the Care Act 2014 requires local authorities to work in person-centred and outcome-focused ways (RiPfA, 2016). Such person-centred and outcome-focused practice with people who self-neglect is supported by:

- shared inter-agency governance arrangements, such as the Safeguarding Adults Board (SAB), which clearly locate strategic responsibility for self-neglect;
- shared definitions and understandings of self-neglect;
- inter-agency coordination and shared risk-management, which is facilitated by clear referral routes, communication and decision-making systems;
- work patterns based on longer-term supportive relationship-based involvement training and supervision which challenge and support practitioners to engage with the ethical challenges, legal options and skills involved in self-neglect practice.

(RiPfA, 2016, p3)

These points are equally relevant for victims of scams who are reluctant or refuse to engage and remain vulnerable to exploitation as they fall 'between active decision makers and those certified as lacking mental capacity' (Sofaer, 2012).

Practice action

Agencies such as trading standards, adult social services, the police and the financial sector may be the first to recognise scamming and be in a position to intervene (Gibson and Qualls, 2012).

Indicators of financial abuse include:

- Changes to physical well-being: weight loss, personal hygiene routines, self-neglect, physical agitation.
- Changes to emotional well-being: low mood, loss of interest in hobbies/activities.
- Reduced contact with family and friends.
- Changes to financial situation: making uncharacteristic financial decisions or a sudden focus on money.
- Increase in post, telephone calls or emails.

Preventative action

The Financial Conduct Authority (FCA, 2014) has produced guidelines to support practitioners to promote scam awareness:

- Do not send advance payments or money to anyone unknown.
- Do not give banking details to anyone unknown.
- Check poor spelling, grammar and check the credentials of the sender.
- Get the Mail Preference Service from Royal Mail.
- Do not give your pin number to anyone.
- Get the Telephone Preference Service.
- Install a call blocker system.
- Do not pay for services in advance.
- Get all arrangements in writing prior to any service.
- Check all credentials.
- Do not deal with cold callers.
- Thoroughly research any offer.

(FCA, 2014, cited in Lee *et al.*, in press)

Why do people get involved with scams?

To develop skills in recognising, protecting and preventing the exploitation of vulnerable people, it is important to understand the characteristics and circumstances which can lead people to respond to scams, or to be targeted: 'their intentions and motivations, their relationship, the nature of the transaction and the degree of harm' (Brown, 2003, p7). The financial abuse and exploitation of others for personal gain shares elements of 'grooming' associated with sexual abuse such as:

> infiltrat[ing] their networks, replacing other more legitimate social contacts (if there are any), with abusers worming their way into positions of trust. These abusers are difficult to challenge because the relationship which is one of exploitation on the part of the abuser may be perceived as a relationship of choice on the part of the vulnerable person.
>
> (Brown, 2003, p6)

Scam involvement is dependent on the individual responding, and the Office of Fair Trading (OFT, 2009) suggests that there is no single risk factor and, in fact, at one point or another, everyone is vulnerable to a persuasive approach but ultimately, the success or failure of a fraud depends on an 'error of judgement on the part of the victim' (OFT, 2009, p24). Depression is cited as a factor in why an individual may respond (Lichtenberg *et al.*, 2013), with chronic financial strain, making a scam more attractive, being associated with poor mental and physical health. The link between loneliness and scam involvement where the regularity of contact and instruction from scammers provides craved-for social contact is discussed in detail in Chapter 4. Theories of human behaviour provide further insight into why some people respond while others do not. These theories shed light on how personality, individual circumstances and personal history interact to make scam involvement more likely (Lee *et al.*, in press). Research by Fischer *et al.* (2013) suggests that there are four key psychological processes encouraging individuals to respond to scams:

- Urgency and scarcity encourages victims to rush decision-making because the offer is time-limited and scarce. Emotive language is used (see Appendix) which excites emotions such as hope and fear and makes emotional control more difficult (Fisher *et al.*, 2013).

- Social influence and consistency creates false rapport and friendships based on 'similarity' with victims. This is a form of grooming. Scammers are adept at making people feel 'special and personally selected' (Lea and Webley, 2006, p21).

- Acceptance of trust cues where scammers imitate authority prompting reciprocation (Cialdini, 1984, cited in Olivier *et al.*, 2015, p361).

- High value incentives invoke responses, and victims are then lured in and hooked by promises of prizes or rewards which are 'nearly' theirs, thus overriding scepticism (Langenderfer and Shimp, 2001). These 'visceral triggers make the victim focus on huge prizes or benefits and imagined positive future emotional states' (Whitty, 2013, p667).

> ### CASE STUDY *2.2*
>
> *Miss A is in her 90s. She is a retired professional who prides herself on never having been in debt. She lives alone and is supported by friends and neighbours who 'look out for her'.*
>
> *Three years ago she purchased a dietary supplement advertised in a free catalogue distributed with her weekly magazine. This led to her being automatically entered into a prize draw. Miss A believed she was close to winning £800,000, which she intended to use to fund her sister's residential care. She consequently purchased more health care products through the catalogue believing this increased her chances of winning. The prize draw was operated in a staged manner and each stage was announced with phrases such as 'guaranteed winner' and with testimonies from previous 'winners'.*
>
> *Since responding to the first prize draw Miss A began receiving up to 10 items of scam post a day from lotteries and prize draws. In addition she received multiple daily telephone calls offering her investment opportunities or informing her she had won a prize (although to claim she had to call a high cost number).*
>
> *After losing a significant amount of money, causing her to alter her lifestyle, Miss A received her 'share' of the prize draw: a cheque for 64p. Miss A realised that this had been a scam and contacted her local trading standards office who provided advice and scam education, including answering scam calls without getting drawn into conversations, thereby managing socialised behaviours of reciprocation.*
>
> *Miss A reported that her experience made her angry at the scammers, but also undermined her confidence in her financial capability.*

Detriment caused by scams

The experience of financial abuse, like other forms of crime such as burglary, can have a severe impact on an individual's health and well-being and their ability to live independently (Donaldson, 2003), and represents a public health concern for the individual and society. Research with victims of financial abuse, supported by intelligence gathered by the National Trading Standards Scams Team, reveals the extensive impact of scams:

Depression and anxiety – Victims of scams which have led to substantial losses have reported that they find the losses emotionally devastating; in some extreme cases victims have attempted or considered suicide.

Anger, resentment, and a sense of betrayal – Felt towards the offender for taking advantage of the victim, especially if they are someone they know.

Social isolation – Victims often suffer their losses in silence rather than risk alienation and societal condemnation if scam involvement is perceived to be the result of their own greed and stupidity.

Stress and pain of victimisation – These may manifest themselves as depression, withdrawal and isolation from family and friends, difficulty at work, and the deterioration of physical and mental health.

Increased vulnerability – To further exploitation.

Inability to replace lost savings – Creating financial anxiety.

Deterioration in physical and mental health – May follow a scam.

Fear – Scams are a personal violation; although there is no serious physical injury, many victims speak of the experience as the psychological equivalent of rape. Victims may fear for their financial security, and express concern about personal safety and well-being.

Self-blame, shame, embarrassment and guilt – May be felt if the victim feels they have contributed to their own or others' victimisation.

Loss of confidence to live independently and loss of self-esteem – A victim's trust in his or her own judgement and trust in others is often shattered. They may hesitate to tell family members, friends or colleagues about their victimisation for fear of criticism. Family members and business associates may even have been financially exploited at the victim's urging, resulting in increased feelings of guilt and blame.

(Adapted from SCIE, 2011a, p11; Whitty, 2013; Button *et al.*, 2014; Age UK, 2015 and unpublished case studies of scam victims collated by the National Trading Standards Scams Team. The Think Jessica Campaign (http://www.thinkjessica.com) provides information, personal experiences and video/photographic evidence of the impact of scams.)

The National Trading Standards Doorstep Crime Project (2015) included a victim impact survey, which highlighted four significant impacts on health and well-being:

- On a scale of 1 to 10, with 10 being the worst effect, 50 per cent rated the effect of the crime on them as between 6 and 10.

- 23 per cent said it had affected their health.

- 38 per cent said it had resulted in them having reduced confidence generally.

- 26 per cent said it had left them feeling down or depressed.

CASE STUDY 2.3

Mrs J is 85. In 2013 she received a letter telling her she had won cash and prizes. After she responded and sent the small fee they requested she started to receive 20–30 letters per day.

(Continued)

CASE STUDY 2.3 *(CONT.)*

'It was at this time that I began to worry about these letters. At the time, I thought the letters were genuine and I could make use of the money as I was beginning to run into debt because of all the letters. I had replied to these companies and included cheques or my debit card details. I also received phone calls from these companies more regularly, throughout the day and late into the evening. Because of this, my health began to get worse. I would go to bed at night worrying about the letters and what would be delivered in the morning. I didn't sleep properly but felt I could not tell anyone as I knew people and my family would tell me I was stupid to get involved with all of this. I became more anxious and generally felt unwell. I still hoped that the prize money would turn up in the near future. I visited the doctor on a number of occasions about my sleep and he was concerned that my blood pressure was high as well. I was prescribed medication regarding this, but still I could not tell anyone.

I continued to enter the draws and order items, and failed to realise that my bank account was now overdrawn by nearly £500. Because of this, I started to feel unwell again and I had very little money for food as I could only just pay my rent, gas and electric bills. My health deteriorated and I then began to receive threatening letters from some of these companies who said that I owed money. I did not understand why as I thought I paid for everything. I felt I had no one to turn to and I was getting more and more in debt. I couldn't sleep and did not know who to turn to. I became anxious when the phone rang as it often was one of these companies asking for money.

I cannot give an exact figure of how much money I have paid out but I ran up an overdraft of nearly £500 and I must have spent thousands on these competitions and clairvoyants. I am still paying back money to the bank.'

Discussion point

Consider how partner agencies can work together to protect individuals like Mrs J.

Economic impact on adult social care

The UK is experiencing increased demand for social care and health services, which are now facing unprecedented fiscal challenges with an anticipated £1.9 billion budget gap in 2016/17 (Humphries *et al.*, 2016). People are living longer and often with complex health needs (POPPI, 2015; Age UK, 2015; Alzheimer's Society, 2014) which makes health prevention a crucial factor in ensuring social care is sustainable in the longer term. This is pertinent to the prevention of financial and material abuse which has personal and national economic impact. Individual financial loss to scams is variable, ranging from a few pounds to many hundreds of thousands lost to scams. The loss may be severe enough to impact on the individual's physical and mental health (Button *et al.*, 2014; Whitty, 2013) resulting in increased need for care and support. In addition the loss of a victim's personal wealth can impact on their ability to fund services to meet their care needs, resulting in ongoing costs to local authorities.

Data are currently unavailable about consequent costs of ongoing care and support needs resulting from financial and material abuse; however, total public expenditure on ASC 2015–16 was £16.97 billion (this figure represents gross current expenditure and includes income from client contributions) (Digital NHS, 2016, p1) and nationally 16 per cent of safeguarding enquiries concern financial and material abuse (Adult Social Care Statistics, 2016). In 2015–16, the average cost of care per adult, per week was £716 for long-term residential care and £596 for long-term nursing care, whilst the average cost of internally provided home care was £30.75 per hour and externally provided home care was £14.28 per hour (Digital NHS, 2016, p1). These figures indicate the potential economic impact on local authority budgets resulting from financial and material abuse from scams.

Key learning points

- Financial abuse from scams is a threat to individual and national health and well-being, often exacerbating or even provoking poor physical or mental health.

- Scams cause significant economic detriment to victims, their communities and national prosperity with implications for adult social care budgets which may have to fund care and support services as a result of increased need and loss of personal wealth.

- People who fall into the gap 'between active decision-makers and those certified as lacking mental capacity' (Sofaer, 2012) may be especially vulnerable to financial exploitation.

- Financial abuse from scams is recognised by safeguarding policy and legislation, but the full extent of its impact on victims has not been a priority in safeguarding practice.

- Inter-agency partnerships around financial abuse offer shared intelligence and expertise.

- The secrecy surrounding financial abuse, under-reporting by victims and issues concerning consent and social expectation regarding inheritance make it difficult for professionals to recognise potentially abusive situations.

Chapter 3

Developing understanding of the nature of scams and the role of trading standards

Louise Baxter and Frances Wilson

CHAPTER OUTCOMES

As a result of completing this chapter you will:

- Understand what financial scams are and the different types of scams which target individuals.

- Understand the scale of the problem caused by scams.

- Be able to identify a range of different scams, including doorstep, mail, telephone and internet scams.

- Understand how financial scammers target their victims, including the language used to entice a response.

- Develop insight of the role of trading standards and the importance of joint working.

Introduction

A 'scam' is a 'trick, a ruse, a swindle, a racket'. Its nearest synonym is 'FRAUD' (Oxford English Dictionary, 2017).

Scams make victims part with their money and personal details by intimidating them or promising cash, prizes, services and fictitious high returns on investments. Scams may be known as mass marketing fraud (misleading or deceptive business practices linked to unsolicited or uninvited contact, for example by letter, email, phone or advertisement in which false promises are made to con the victim out of their money) or doorstep crime (scams occurring on the doorstep of a person's home).

Words such as 'scam', 'con', 'swindle', 'bamboozle' and 'cheat' are sometimes used to describe fraud. The slang nature of these terms hide the seriousness of the crimes they represent. The effects of fraud can be extremely harmful, not only depriving individuals and businesses of their money, but can also include social harms and trauma (National Fraud Authority, 2013, p3). No matter what we call them it is important to remember that scams are crimes. The word 'scam' not only minimises the perceived financial detriment and personal impact a consumer experiences, but also gives a sense that there is a level of culpability or contributory negligence. This can decrease the already low probability of such a fraud being reported and may explain why, it is estimated, only 5 per cent of victims report being scammed (Office of Fair Trading, 2006).

The NTS Scams Team wants to change the perception of the word scam as currently it does not resonate with the general public nor illustrate the serious impact of the fraud these victims suffer. Through the Friends Against Scams initiative (see below) the team will improve the public's understanding that scams represent a crime.

The scale of the problem

Each year scams cause between £5 and £10 billion of detriment to UK consumers (NTS Scams Team, 2015). A 2013 estimate by the former National Fraud Authority (NFA) put total losses for individuals at over £9 billion per annum. This is a useful indicator, but is likely to be a significant under-estimate due to under-reporting and the fact that it may not include every type of fraud. The NFA based its estimates on the scale of mass marketing fraud, identity fraud, online ticket fraud, private rental property fraud and electricity prepayment meter scams (National Fraud Authority, 2013). Doorstep scams were not considered by the NFA.

Scams have a substantial impact on economies and markets by undermining consumer trust in legitimate businesses. The Office of Fair Trading (2006) reports that 'more than half of [United Kingdom] scam victims admitted to having changed their purchasing and payment behaviour, generally becoming more cautious or suspicious of any contact that could potentially be another scam' (OFT, 2006, p25).

Mass marketing scams are not an issue in the UK alone, but are a pervasive global criminal threat. There are strong indications that the order of magnitude of global mass marketing fraud losses is in the tens of billions of dollars per year. For example, in 2016 the United States Treasury Department deemed a Canadian payment processing company associated with international mass marketing fraud to be a 'significant transnational criminal organisation' (US Treasury, 2016), landing it on the same short-list as some of the world's most notorious mobsters, racketeers, drug cartels and murderers.

The scale of the problem should not be underestimated; Age UK found that 53 per cent of people aged 65 or over believe they have been targeted by fraudsters (Age UK, 2015). In some cases consumers aged 70+ have had to re-mortgage or sell their homes or take out loans to cover debts they incur due to scams. Whilst only 1 in 12 responded to the scam, 70 per cent of people of all age groups who did respond said that they had personally lost money. This could mean that a staggering half a million older people have fallen victim to losing savings. Recent reforms to private pensions make it likely that people retiring will be targeted by fraudsters who know that they can now draw all their pensions in cash.

It is believed that 3.2 million adults, one person in every 15, have fallen victim to scams each year and around a third of all scam victims will fall prey to another scam within 12 months. Most worryingly research exploring the experience of burglary victims found that adults who are defrauded in their own homes are two and a half times more likely to either die or go into residential care within a year of the fraud occurring than those who have not (National Trading Standards Doorstep Crime Project Report 2014/15, March 2015). These statistics show that it is vital that more work is done to protect potentially vulnerable people from the financial and emotional devastation scams cause. Part of this work is ensuring a greater understanding of what scams are and why people respond to them.

CASE STUDY 3.1

A husband and wife, both 65 years old, together lost more than £1 million to an inheritance scam being operated out of China, the Netherlands and Spain. The couple used their life savings, re-financed their home and withdrew retirement funds to pay for the advance fees that the scheme charged. As a result of the losses, the wife has attempted suicide twice. The couple then lost their home to foreclosure and were both treated for depression.

How to recognise scams and types of mass marketing scams

The biggest sign that something is a scam is if a person or organisation you do not know or have not heard of before asks you for money. The most common types of scams that the NTS Scams Team encounter are lottery or prize draw scams, clairvoyants and doorstep scams.

Lottery or prize draw scams

These scams claim the recipient has won a large sum of money or high value goods in a competition or lottery they did not enter and a fee is required to release the prize. This fee is disguised as a 'processing' or 'admin' fee to allegedly cover either the tax associated with the winnings or as a cost of running the contest. The victim has not won any prize and will continue to receive letters asking them for more and more small amounts of money to cover other supposed fees.

Clairvoyants

These scams claim to offer protection from bad spirits or offer energy to the recipient. The victims are encouraged to send money to the clairvoyant either as a gesture of thanks for the help offered or in order to buy a 'sacred' item that will protect the victim. Victims may be groomed over time, leading to a relationship forming in which the victim has invested both emotionally and financially, and may be reluctant to end. There is no tangible evidence to suggest that certain groups of people are more vulnerable to these types of scams. However, the NTS Scams Team has anecdotal evidence suggesting that those who have suffered a recent loss or bereavement may be more likely to respond.

Figure 3.1 Example of scam mailings.

Figure 3.2 Examples of protective talismans sent by clairvoyants.

ACTIVITY 3.1

How to recognise scam mail

Study the example of scam mail below (Figure 3.3) and see if you can spot any signs that it may be a scam or why you may be tempted to respond.

Signs of the scam

The letter is always addressed to the victim; junk mail will be addressed to 'The Homeowner' while scam mail will be to 'Mrs K Smith'. The victim's name is used throughout the letter to make it appear more personal.

The letter, and often the envelope, will be very colourful and often gaudy to make it enticing to the victim. There will be many stamps and seals proclaiming the integrity of the letter and it will often feature the signature of the 'Director' or 'Chief Officer' to make it seem more official.

The letters will put the recipient under pressure to respond quickly so that they don't have time to consider if the offer really is too good to be true.

The return address will be a PO Box number abroad. If you compare the return addresses of several scams you will see that many of them have incredibly similar addresses. This is because the letters are not sent to the glamorous headquarters of a luxury lotto firm or the mystic home of a clairvoyant, but to a post office box on an industrial estate.

There will often be messages advising the recipient to keep the letters a secret from family and friends as they will only become jealous or want to stop the victim's good luck.

This can make the scam victim more dependent on the criminal and prevents the victim from feeling comfortable asking another person for a second opinion.

The letters will ask the recipient for money or bank details.

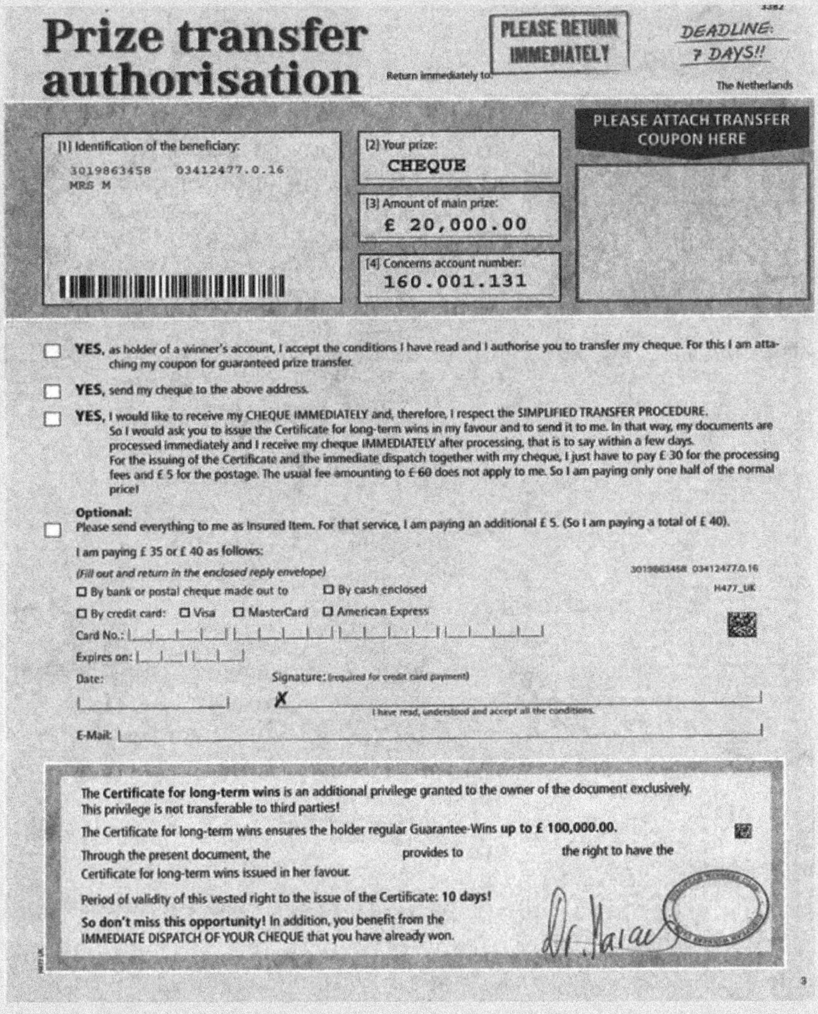

Prize transfer authorisation

Return immediately to:

PLEASE RETURN IMMEDIATELY

DEADLINE: 7 DAYS!!

The Netherlands

PLEASE ATTACH TRANSFER COUPON HERE

[1] Identification of the beneficiary:
3019863458 03412477.0.16
MRS M

[2] Your prize:
CHEQUE

[3] Amount of main prize:
£ 20,000.00

[4] Concerns account number:
160.001.131

☐ **YES,** as holder of a winner's account, I accept the conditions I have read and I authorise you to transfer my cheque. For this I am attaching my coupon for guaranteed prize transfer.

☐ **YES,** send my cheque to the above address.

☐ **YES,** I would like to receive my CHEQUE IMMEDIATELY and, therefore, I respect the SIMPLIFIED TRANSFER PROCEDURE.
So I would ask you to issue the Certificate for long-term wins in my favour and to send it to me. In that way, my documents are processed immediately and I receive my cheque IMMEDIATELY after processing, that is to say within a few days.
For the issuing of the Certificate and the immediate dispatch together with my cheque, I just have to pay £ 30 for the processing fees and £ 5 for the postage. The usual fee amounting to £ 60 does not apply to me. So I am paying only one half of the normal price!

Optional:
☐ Please send everything to me as Insured Item. For that service, I am paying an additional £ 5. (So I am paying a total of £ 40).

I am paying £ 35 or £ 40 as follows:
(Fill out and return in the enclosed reply envelope) 3019863458 03412477.0.16
☐ By bank or postal cheque made out to ☐ By cash enclosed H477_UK
☐ By credit card: ☐ Visa ☐ MasterCard ☐ American Express
Card No.:
Expires on:
Date:
Signature: (required for credit card payment)
✗
I have read, understood and accept all the conditions.
E-Mail:

The **Certificate for long-term wins** is an additional privilege granted to the owner of the document exclusively.
This privilege is not transferable to third parties!
The Certificate for long-term wins ensures the holder regular Guarantee-Wins **up to £ 100,000.00.**
Through the present document, the provides to the right to have the Certificate for long-term wins issued in her favour.
Period of validity of this vested right to the issue of the Certificate: **10 days!**
So don't miss this opportunity! In addition, you benefit from the IMMEDIATE DISPATCH OF YOUR CHEQUE that you have already won.

Dr. Haiau

3

Figure 3.3 Example of a scam letter.

ACTIVITY 3.2

How to recognise a scam email

Study the example of a scam email below and see if you can spot any signs that it may be a scam or why you may be tempted to respond.

(Continued)

From: **MRS. E.** <hmrc.refund@intelelite.info>

Date: 8 June 2016 at 16:33

Subject: contact Western Union Office

To:

Good day,

We have deposited your fund of $2.5 million usd dollars through Western Union department after our finally meeting regarding your fund, All you will do is to contact western union director Pastor Terry Cool (western_money_transfer@outlook.com) He will give you direction on how you will be receiving the funds daily. My agreement with them is $5000 daily until the whole funds is transferred to you. Contact western union director Terry Cool send him your Full information to avoid wrong transfer such as,

Receiver's Name ....

Adress ......

Country .....

Phone Number .....

Though, Terry cool has sent $5000 in your name today so contac Terry Cool or you call him +229-62258844 as soon as you receive this email and tell him to give you the Mtcn, sender name and question/answer to picj the $5000. Please let us know as soon as you received all your fund, Best Regards.

MRS. E.

Signs of the scam

The email will not be addressed to the victim personally. This is because a criminal can send the same email to hundreds of people and blind copy them all in to save time. If they addressed the recipient by name then they would have to spend more time sending out individual emails. Often the emails will open 'Dear Friend' or 'Valued Customer'.

The language and grammar in scam emails is often terrible; this is partly because the criminals behind the emails do not speak English as their primary language, but it is also down to other factors: broken or misspelt English may allow the email to get past a user's spam filters. More experienced internet users may see the email and immediately dismiss it as a scam, but those who do respond are more likely to respond with greater amounts of money.

The emails will often contain a subject header that bears no relevance to the content of the email. The email address will often not match the organisation the email is purporting to be from. In all cases there will be pressure to respond immediately and a request for personal or banking details as in scam mail.

Doorstep scams

These scams occur when a person is cold-called at their home and persuaded to part with money for home repairs or garden work that is unnecessary. If the work is completed it will be to a very poor standard or the criminals may take the victim's money and leave the work incomplete. An extortionate price is nearly always charged. Often what is quoted as a small and low cost piece of work will escalate into an expensive job that takes many weeks. It can be difficult for the victim to recognise it is a scam as the criminals will be very convincing and will state that they are offering the victim a great deal. Doorstep scams can be particularly devastating to people as they may no longer feel safe in their own home.

CASE STUDY 3.2

Mrs K had been diagnosed with dementia and was living alone as all her family lived several hundred miles away. Her doctors were happy for her to stay in her home as they believed she could become distressed if she had to move away. A man called at the house offering to repair her roof as the tiles were supposedly damaged. He stated that the work would cost around £500.

Over the following months he continued to visit Mrs K and demand more and more money from her until she had paid over £6,000. When she told him that she did not have any more money he forced his way into her home and threatened to steal an antique clock that her late husband had given her to pay for the work. Trading standards were alerted and tried to catch the criminal but he had already left the premises. They estimated that the work done was only worth £25.

The experience was so traumatising for Mrs K that she immediately left her home and moved into a care home. She is very unhappy in the care home as she misses her friends in the village, her garden and the familiar environment of her home; these were anchors in her life that, despite her dementia, were allowing her to live independently.

Signs that someone may be being scammed

- High volume of scam mail.
- Lots of cheap 'tat' and hoarding.
- Poor living conditions/poor personal hygiene.
- High usage of cheque books.
- Frequent visits to the bank or post office.
- Not paying bills or buying food.
- Unusual/unexplained bank account activity.
- Deceitful about scam participation.

- Secretive about their relationships.
- Increasing isolation from family/friends.
- High volume of phone calls.
- Talk about a caller as their 'friend'.

How do scammers target people?

When the criminals send out scam mail or contact someone via the telephone, the communications will always be personal and addressed to a specific person. This can make the claims of prize winnings or great opportunities seem more believable. They are not addressed 'To the occupier' as junk mail is. How do the criminals obtain people's personal information in order to target them so effectively? Criminals will buy data lists from each other, often called 'suckers lists', that contain all the information they need to effectively target someone, including: name, address, age, possible health issues, what scams a person has previously responded to and how much they have spent.

After a raid on the headquarters of an organisation that was involved in scams, investigators found meticulous records had been kept of how much, and when each victim had sent money in. This information not only allowed the organisation to target victims effectively, but also created an extra revenue stream as the data were incredibly valuable to other scam organisations.

Criminals may also buy their mailing lists from legitimate data brokers who build up mailing lists when people agree to allow their data to be shared or sold on (NTS Scams Team intelligence). In one case a 67-year-old woman responded to an advertisement in a national newspaper for a knee support. Within two weeks of responding she received four letters telling her she had won an international lottery and would receive her winnings if she just paid a small release fee (trading standards case study).

REFLECTION 3.1

Consider how many mailing lists (either email or physical post) that you have signed up to. Do you know if you have allowed the people behind these lists to share your data with others?

How often do you remember to check the data sharing box when you fill out a form with your personal information on it? Does the box mean you are opting in or are you opting out of data sharing?

How do scammers appeal to people?

A common misconception about those who respond to scams is that they are stupid and greedy. As discussed in Chapter 2, scammers exploit fundamental human behaviours, needs and desires, and research by the University of Portsmouth (Button *et al.*, 2014) and the National Fraud Authority found that 'greed' and 'stupidity' were rarely factors in whether people became victims of fraud. Letters from victims to the NTS Scams Team reveal that in many cases the victims wanted the money in order to spend it on friends and family or even essential medical treatments.

Scams look genuine – Criminals work hard to make scams look legitimate and official; therefore, people are more inclined to trust authority.

High value rewards – By offering life changing money for a relatively small initial outlay, criminals entice victims into responding. They are encouraged to feel they have little to lose and possibly much to gain.

Exploitation of wants and needs – Criminals prey on the universal human desire to want the most out of life. They offer the guarantee of great wealth, good fortune, cures for ill health, weight loss and generally a better life. As a result less time is spent on checking the legitimacy of the claim because people naturally want it to be true.

Personalised mail – Many people who are targeted by criminals do not realise how easy it is to personalise correspondence. Equally they are unaware of the amount of information that exists about them and the ease with which it can be accessed or shared. They falsely give credence to a scam approach because they believe that a great deal of time has been spent in writing exclusively to them. They cannot comprehend a scammer would be able to send off hundreds of letters a day.

False timescales – By making false deadlines criminals force victims to react quickly before they have had time to reflect and properly consider the merits of participation.

Active participation – Criminals encourage the victim to engage from an early stage by making them tick boxes, place stickers on forms and fill out information. As the victim has invested time and money they are more likely to commit to the relationship. This makes it easier for criminals to request further sums of money or information.

Secrecy – By promoting an environment of secrecy the scammer prevents a victim from taking advice from their family and/or friends, which makes them easier to manipulate.

Many people believe that they would be able to spot a scam and know not to respond; however, the criminals behind scams are very clever and use manipulative, persuasive language to ensure that they get a response. In some cases, particularly clairvoyants, they may prey on a person's fears; for example '… an abnormal presence around you, as if a negative influence was trying to drag your life into a downward spiral. We will need to be careful with certain people around you. This is so that you stop things getting worse and worse.' This language implies that the criminal is there to help the victim while at the same time alienating them from anyone who may be able to offer support. With lottery or prize draw scams the victim is told that they have won money or a prize. Phrases such as 'confirmed winner', 'lucky recipient' or 'winning claim' feature heavily in these types of scams. The victim does not believe that they are taking a risk in sending money as the letters they have received have confirmed to them that they are a winner.

ACTIVITY 3.3

Use the internet to research prize draws. Compare the language used in the legitimate promotions with the following excerpt from a scam prize draw:

'One look at your customer file tells me you have the ability to recognise a great lotto opportunity when you see it. So I know the news that follows will, quite rightly, leave you with a delightful buzz of anticipation. Indeed, by the time you've finished reading, you'll probably feel like you can almost touch the money.'

'Then something terribly exciting happened – when the free bonus assessment took place as per the President's order the board's unanimous decision was that your free bonus should be BOOSTED! That's right you passed the assessment with flying colours and your free bonuses allocation went sky high!'

'This Financial update requires your immediate attention. To claim prize opportunity you must act within 14 days.'

Which is the more alluring or implies the greater chance of success?

Why are older people targeted by scams?

Data gathered by the National Scams Team about scam victims, along with details contained in 'suckers lists', suggests that the average age of a scam victim is 75 years old. With recent changes to private pensions allowing people aged 55+ to take all their pension savings in cash it is likely that the scammers will target this age group even more.

Availability – It is likely that older people are retired and may be less mobile. As a consequence, they will spend a higher proportion of their time at home. This makes it easier for criminals responsible for scams to initially contact and sustain a period of manipulation.

Awareness – In some cases, older people may suffer from a decline in cognitive functioning, which can lead to poor decision-making resulting in decreased ability to calculate risks. This can make older people particularly vulnerable to criminals responsible for scams which provide misleading or inadequate information from the outset. Criminals often rely on victims being confused in order to dupe them out of their money. In 2015 dementia became the biggest cause of death in England and Wales according to the Office for National Statistics. It is predicted that by 2025 there will be more than one million people living with dementia in the UK and it is likely that criminals will take advantage of the increased number of people with cognitive decline. This subject is discussed in detail in Chapter 5.

Social isolation – According to a study by Age UK (2014) nearly half (49 per cent) of all people aged 75 and over live alone and 17 per cent of older people have less than weekly contact with family, friends and neighbours. We can see from this that many scam victims could be incredibly isolated and the contact they have with scammers may be the only contact they have with anyone that day, or even that week. 'The worst part of old age is the loneliness' (letter from a victim to a scammer). Many victims do not have the support network to gain a second opinion from a friend or family member about a phone call or letter that they have received and will believe the words of the criminals as they have no one else to challenge it.

Loneliness – Evidence links loneliness with deteriorating health and well-being (discussed in detail in Chapter 4). Around a million (10 per cent) older people are termed 'chronically lonely' at any given time in the UK (LGA, 2016), which will seriously increase their risk of suffering mental and physical illness. Loneliness also puts individuals at greater risk of cognitive decline, which is a key factor that contributes to becoming a victim of a scam. Lonely scam victims often engage with a scammer more readily than other people because of the natural need for human interaction. In addition to the personal suffering caused by loneliness it is adding pressure to council and health services, as it is often the tipping point for referrals to adult social care and cause for a significant number of GP visits (LGA, 2016c, p2).

Perception that older people have more available wealth – The prime motivation of most, if not all criminals, responsible for scams is the pursuit of financial gain. Potentially older people may have accumulated substantial levels of wealth over their lifetime in the form of savings, property and other assets. Many victims become unwitting participants in scams through a desire to help their families by, for example, providing a windfall, clearing a mortgage or funding a grandchild's university education. As a result they are happy to utilise their high levels of disposable income to receive the promised windfall.

CASE STUDY **3.3**

Mr and Mrs A had been scam victims for around 20 years. They had run a successful leisure business for many years and were financially stable. Then, around 20 years ago, the business started to fail.

Mr A:

'When the first letters came telling me I'd won large sums of money I thought it could be true and just what I needed as I'd lost so much money because of the effect on our business. I suppose the scammers caught me at a low ebb.'

(Continued)

CASE STUDY *3.3* (CONT.)

When the situation was at its worst they were sending £300 in cash a week to the criminals. Over the years their son had tried to convince them that they were responding to scams and not genuine lotteries or prize draws but to no avail. The problem was so severe that their son was afraid his parents wouldn't be able to pay their household bills.

Mrs A helped Mr A reply to the letters and became heavily involved too. So much so that when Mrs A started to show signs of dementia, Mr A felt that the administrative work involved with replying to scams would keep his wife's mind sharp; she continued to do this until it all got too much for her and she was no longer able to deal with it because of her condition.

When trading standards intervened Mr A realised the mail was scam mail. He took advantage of the mail redirection service so all the mail was redirected to their son.

After two weeks Mr A's son said:

'Progress has been excellent. I get all the scam mail now and have had 20 items in the past two days. Nothing reaches my parents now and for the first time in a long time I can see that there is more money going into my father's account than going out. The only money going out is to pay household bills. It's such a relief.'

It is important to note that Mr and Mrs A started to respond to scams during a period of vulnerability – the decline of their business.

*Mr A's son estimates that his parents had been scammed to the tune of **well over a £100,000** over the years.*

Role of trading standards and importance of joint working

As discussed in Chapter 7, trading standards plays a major role in identifying and supporting victims of scams. As with most cases involving the protection of potentially vulnerable people, trading standards officers have found that there is not a single approach to supporting victims of scams. Each case must be assessed on the needs and personality of the victim. Some victims may respond to a formal approach to 'shock' them into understanding that the mail they are responding to is fraudulent. In one case a couple only stopped responding to scam mail when a police officer accompanied the trading standards officer on their visit and told the couple that they were at risk of being charged with money laundering if they continued to respond to the letters. However, others may respond more positively to an informal approach. In Northern Ireland one victim was convinced that the letters were fraudulent after just one visit from trading standards officers. After discussion Mrs B broke down on the doorstep and she told the officer that she had lost at least £10,000. Mrs B asked the officer why they had not seen her years ago as it would have saved her thousands of pounds (NTS Scams Team case study). In this instance the trading standards officer was able to spend time sorting through the victim's post and explaining to her that the clairvoyants she had been responding to were criminals. It is vital that scam prevention strategies and interventions are carried out with partner agencies such as charities specialising in older adults or adult social care, as victims often require the support of services that trading standards cannot offer. This can best be seen in the case of Mr J in Case Study 3.4.

CASE STUDY 3.4

Mr J was an 83-year-old man who had lost his partner in tragic circumstances; due to this loss Mr J was at a particularly vulnerable point in his life. Trading standards were alerted by the bank regarding suspicious transactions on Mr J's account. Mr J repeatedly refused to explain these transactions or engage with those wishing to help him. It was clear a crime was taking place, but the nature of the crime was not clear. Mr J's bank called trading standards on at least five occasions raising concerns about the activity on his account before Mr J finally permitted officers entry to his home. When officers did enter his home they found him to be living in squalid conditions. His house was freezing and was stacked full of boxes, parcels and piles of mail. It was complete mayhem apart from an ordered dining room table, which had a precise filing system of letters containing fraudulent attempts at extracting money from a vulnerable man. Mr J was very protective of his letters and guarded them fiercely.

Mr J eventually admitted to the officers that he was sending money abroad in order to release lottery winnings. Over a number of years he had sent more money than he could recall to fraudsters purporting to be the administrators of a large lottery win. By now he had spent everything – his credit card was at its limit, he was overdrawn and penniless. He was preparing to sign over his home. Due to the joint working of trading standards and social workers a safeguarding plan was immediately put into action; within 24 hours electricity was restored to Mr J's home, the heating was back on and meals on wheels had been engaged to deliver hot food to Mr J. Social workers assessed Mr J and decided that he did not have mental capacity and the decision was made for his own protection to redirect his mail to a covert trading standards mailbox and install a call blocking system to block 'unwanted' telephone calls. The fraudsters continued to target Mr J; mail poured into the trading standards post box and over 300 calls were made to him, but the call blocking device prevented these calls reaching him and the scam mail was never passed on to him. Mr J was warm, fed and his living conditions dramatically improved.

Mr J's case demonstrates the importance of joint agency working. Without the direct involvement of social workers it is unlikely that immediate action could have taken place. In Croydon a formal joint working protocol is in place to ensure that it is not left to chance in future cases. Regular training sessions are organised for care professionals (such as occupational therapists, GPs, nurses, the third sector, police) to ensure that safeguarding of potentially vulnerable people becomes a collaborative issue.

Joint working is not limited to the involvement of the social care sector. In Hampshire and Lincolnshire trading standards work closely with the local police to ensure residents are protected. Police community support officers (PCSOs) in Lincolnshire have received special training in how to recognise scams and scam victims. In East Sussex trading standards has partnered with the local branch of Age UK to provide support to scam victims, and Age UK are able to provide a holistic approach to protecting and supporting potentially vulnerable people.

Alongside joint working it is important for local authorities to engage with other partners for educational opportunities. In Reading and Birmingham trading standards officers have worked closely with local Girl Guiding and Scouts Associations to deliver scams awareness talks to younger age groups to raise awareness of financial fraud and the impact on victims. This can help spread information to grandparents about the nature of scams.

Trading standards and the Care Act 2014

Section 42 of the Care Act 2014 requires local authorities to make enquires, or ask others to make enquiries, when they think an adult with care and support needs may be at risk of abuse or neglect in their area and to find out what, if any, action may be needed. As discussed in Chapter 2, scams and fraud are identified by the Care Act 2014 as forms of financial abuse. Currently the National Trading Standards Scams Team has just under 300,000 confirmed and potential scam victims in its database, the average age of whom is 75. Whilst age does not necessarily indicate vulnerability to scam involvement, it is related to other factors which can result in vulnerability, such as dementia and loneliness (as discussed in Chapters 4 and 5).

Underpinning the Care Act is the well-being principle, a broad concept which the Act relates to nine specific domains. Of particular relevance to scamming are the following domains:

- personal dignity (including treatment of the individual with respect);
- physical and mental health and emotional well-being;
- protection from abuse and neglect.

The well-being principle requires local authorities to provide or arrange services that help prevent people developing needs for care and support. In light of the growing body of knowledge about the detriment to people's health and well-being caused by involvement in scams, prevention strategies interventions should include a focus on scam and fraud prevention.

The Care Act 2014 statutory guidance (2016) recognises that trading standards have a valuable contribution to make in ensuring adults are safeguarded:

14.28 Internet scams, postal scams and doorstep crime are more often than not targeted at adults at risk and all are forms of financial abuse. These scams are becoming ever more sophisticated and elaborate. For example:

- *Internet scammers can build very convincing websites.*

- *People can be referred to a website to check the caller's legitimacy but this may be a copy of a legitimate website.*

- *Postal scams are mass-produced letters which are made to look like personal letters or important documents.*

- *Doorstep criminals call unannounced at the adult's home under the guise of legitimate business and offer to fix an often non-existent problem with their property. Sometimes they pose as police officers or someone in a position of authority.*

14.29 In all cases this is financial abuse and the adult at risk can be persuaded to part with large sums of money and in some cases their life savings. These instances should always be reported to the local police service and local authority trading standards services for investigation. The Safeguarding Adults Board will need to consider how to involve local trading standards in its work.

14.30 These scams and crimes can seriously affect the health, including mental health, of an adult at risk. Agencies working together can better protect adults at risk. Failure to do so can result in an increased cost to the state, especially if the adult at risk loses their income and independence.

Safeguarding adults with care needs who are subject to financial abuse via scams therefore need to be considered as part of a whole council and indeed whole partnership approach.

Conclusion

The scale of the problem posed by scams is immense, and with an ageing population that has early access to their pension funds, it is likely that the problem will continue to grow. It is now more important than ever for those with safeguarding responsibilities to work together to protect potential victims from scams and to increase awareness of the issue through the education of communities. Across the country local authorities are developing innovative ways of supporting scam victims and are increasing joint working practices. The NTS Scams Team believes that these practices need to become the standard way of working and formal joint working plans should be put in place to ensure it is not left to chance that victims receive support from all departments.

Although local authorities should not become reliant on charities or volunteer services to meet their statutory responsibilities, partnership work with third sector organisations that provide support and information for specific populations is a valuable way of addressing need. Charities such as Age UK may be able to assist local authorities by offering a holistic range of services that can support victims. Additionally many third sector organisations deliver education and awareness courses to their volunteers or their local communities; these can be an excellent opportunity to increase scams awareness and educate individuals and communities on how to protect themselves. There is compelling evidence that older people and other vulnerable individuals are being targeted by criminals with scams. Furthermore, the percentage population at risk of falling victim is steadily increasing. Without strong interventions to prevent their victimisation the consequences are severe in terms of increased health needs and support.

Key learning points

- There are numerous ways in which scammers can target individuals including at the doorstep, and through the mail, telephone and internet. The aim of all of these approaches is to take money from the victim.

- It is estimated that the financial scale of detriment caused by scams in the UK is between £5 and £10 billion annually.

- Scam mail is often created to look official, or to appear as a genuine offer. For example, lotteries or competitions may look genuine, but closer inspection of the language used, spelling mistakes etc. are often giveaway clues of scam mail.

- Scammers manipulate their contact with people to exploit certain vulnerabilities, such as loneliness and cognitive impairment, to increase the likelihood of the individual responding to a scam.

- Trading standards have an essential role in identifying and supporting victims of scams. They are therefore a central element of partnership work in adult safeguarding activity.

- It is important that adult safeguarding activity concerned with combating financial scams involves joint working across a number of key agencies including trading standards, local authorities, health and the police.

Chapter 4
Loneliness, well-being and scam involvement

Lee-Ann Fenge

CHAPTER OUTCOMES

As a result of completing this chapter you will:

- Understand the differences between loneliness and social isolation.

- Understand the impact of loneliness on health and well-being.

- Understand how loneliness may be an important consideration in terms of promoting well-being as defined by the Care Act.

- Understand how loneliness may lead some individuals to be at increased risk of involvement in financial scams.

Introduction

This chapter sets out to consider how loneliness and social isolation may act as risk factors for involvement in financial scams. This is an important topic to explore as loneliness is one of the main indicators of social well-being, and health and social care practitioners often work with individuals who present as lonely or socially isolated. It is therefore important that public services, and health and social care practitioners, consider how loneliness may compromise well-being and increase vulnerability to financial abuse and financial scams.

As Chapter 1 indicated, within the Care Act 2014 well-being should be seen as the common theme around which care and support is built at both local and national levels (Care Act 2014; Guidance, 2016). Practitioners need knowledge and understanding of the duties agencies now have as a result of the Care Act 2014 to safeguard individuals from financial abuse, and this is important as financial abuse is the second most common form of abuse experienced by vulnerable adults (Biggs *et al.*, 2009). The well-being principle applies in all cases where a local authority is carrying out a care and support function, or making a decision, and as part of this it is important to understand how loneliness and social isolation may negatively impact upon an individual's overall well-being. It is also important to consider how an understanding of the impact of loneliness and social isolation on well-being may inform the development of personalised safeguarding using the six safeguarding principles outlined by the Department of Health (DH, 2013). These principles include:

- Empowerment

- Partnership

- Protection

- Prevention

- Proportionality

- Accountability.

For example, the principles of empowerment and prevention might include equipping individuals with opportunities to improve financial literacy to become more scam-aware. This in turn may enable individuals to safeguard themselves from the risks of financial scam involvement. The National Trading Standards (NTS) Scams Team recently launched a new initiative which aims to protect and prevent people from becoming victims of scams by empowering communities to 'Take a Stand Against Scams'. For more information on this see **www.friendsagainstscams.org.uk**.

Why is loneliness an important topic for those involved in safeguarding adults at risk of harm? Increasingly loneliness is a concern for health and social care agencies as it can be 'a tipping point' for an individual being referred to adult social care or being seen regularly at GP surgeries (LGA, 2016c, p2). This is not just a problem within the UK, but is a global challenge; social isolation and loneliness in later life are global issues and have been identified across a range of different countries and cultures (Chen *et al.*, 2014). Loneliness can occur at any time during our lives, but may become more acute due to increased emotional vulnerability as a result of life events such as illness or bereavement. Such life events may become more prevalent in later life as a result of the death of a partner, or chronic illness. For example, 3 in 10 people aged over 80 report feelings of loneliness, which is higher than any other age group (Office for National Statistics, 2015). The Doorstep Crime Project Report 2014/15 found that 57 per cent of the people who reported doorstep scams lived alone, 41 per cent felt lonely and 34 per cent had experienced recent bereavement (National Trading Standards Board, 2015). Therefore it appears that increased emotional vulnerability due to loneliness may increase susceptibility to scams involvement (Olivier *et al.*, 2015).

To begin with, the chapter will explore what loneliness is, and considers the relationship between loneliness and social isolation. The chapter will then consider what loneliness means for those with specific needs, before considering how loneliness might predispose someone to respond to a scam.

How do we define loneliness?

Loneliness is an experience that all of us can probably relate to, and at certain points in our lives we may encounter feelings of loneliness. It is a subjective feeling and does not necessarily relate to having no social connections or relationships, and indeed it can be possible to feel lonely in a crowd or group. Living alone does not necessarily lead to loneliness and there is a clear difference between loneliness, which is a subjective term, and social isolation, which is an objective term and relates to a lack of social contacts or connections.

People experience loneliness in different ways and it is a social problem which can have an impact on an individual's health, well-being and quality of life (Dury, 2014). Loneliness is therefore related to how an individual perceives their social relationships rather than a complete absence of social relationships. Feeling lonely can have a negative impact on our emotional state, and this results from a difference between desired and achieved levels of social contact (Peplau and Perlman, 1982). Loneliness has been defined as a 'distressing feeling that accompanies the perception that one's social needs are not being met by the quantity or especially the quality of one's social relationships' (Hawkley and Cacioppo, 2010, p218). Loneliness is related to both physical and mental well-being, and the distress caused by loneliness has been found to be a risk factor for increased morbidity (Penninx *et al.*, 1999) and mortality (Luo *et al.*, 2012).

Everyone can experience loneliness at different points in their life; sometimes this may be a transient experience and sometimes it may become a chronic feeling which has a longer lasting impact. However, some individuals may be at increased risk of feelings of loneliness due to factors such as age, mental and physical health status, finances, housing, ethnicity and gender. For example, research with people who have mental health conditions suggests that loneliness is experienced as both emotionally and socially excluding (Lindgren *et al.*, 2014).

Social isolation is an objective term which describes an absence of contact with others including family, friends and the community. It is therefore more of a description of circumstances than a perceived experience. People who are socially isolated from their community are more likely to feel lonely, but people who feel lonely may not be socially isolated. The experience of being lonely is more prevalent and can have bigger implications on health and well-being than social isolation (Luo *et al.*, 2012). Loneliness is therefore not synonymous with social isolation, but is related to both the amount of social contact (quantity) as well as the features (quality) of social relationships. As the above descriptions indicate, loneliness and social isolation are not the same thing, but are clearly linked. Social exclusion is a term which has also been linked to increased feelings of loneliness (Kneale, 2012) and the experience of social exclusion can be characterised by seven domains:

- social relationships;
- cultural factors;

- civic activities and access to information;

- local amenities;

- decent housing and public transport;

- common consumer goods; and

- financial products.

It is therefore important to view the individual within their wider social and community system as this can exert an influence on their experience of exclusion and social isolation, and their perceived experience of loneliness. As part of this it is important to consider how changes in social care policy, such as a move towards personalised care and individual budgets, may isolate vulnerable individuals further. This concern has been highlighted in a study by Manthorpe *et al.* (2009) which identifies the potential vulnerability of some people using individual budgets to exploitation.

It is important to remember that when describing their lives individuals will probably not distinguish between the terms loneliness and social isolation. What is important to them is the lived experience rather than the definition attached to it. When working with individuals in a safeguarding context it may be helpful to develop a pictorial representation of the person within their wider social context, and this may help to illuminate what social connections they have, with whom and the social support they may or may not receive from the wider community. The Ecological Model proposed by Bronfenbrenner (1979, cited by Galpin, 2016, pp128–130) is a useful tool when exploring loneliness as it focuses on the level of connectedness within an individual's environment. This model proposes the following five levels within an individual's environmental system:

- **Microsystem** – those that have a direct contact with the individual and operate as bi-directional influences. A scam perpetrator could certainly develop direct contact with an individual, which is played out over time as a 'friendship' with the scammer is developed.

- **Mesosystem** – this involves the linkages between the different microsystems which affect the individual. For example, it might relate to links between their family, social care providers and GP services.

- **Exosystem** – more general level which indirectly affect interactions. For example, this might include adult children that live at a distance and therefore have only minimal contact with an ageing parent, limiting their ability to offer informal care.

- **Macrosystem** – this includes wider societal influences, such as political, social, cultural and economic values within society. The experience of marginalisation and discrimination may exert an influence on loneliness in terms of discrimination as the result of ageism, racism, disablism, heterosexism etc.

- **Chronosystem** – this relates to changes which occur over time, for example retirement, bereavement, changes in family structure. These key life transitions can upset an individual's equilibrium and trigger feelings of loneliness.

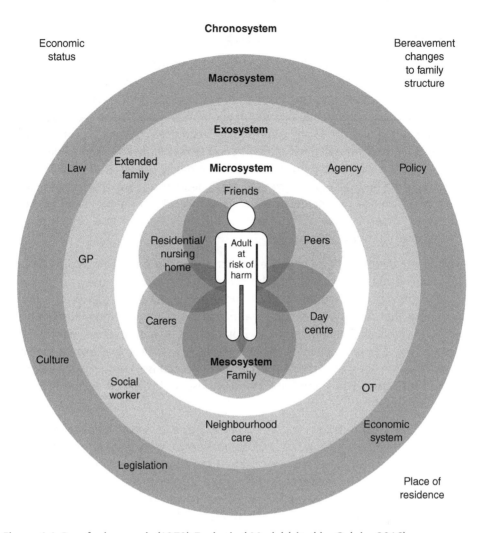

Figure 4.1 Bronfenbrenner's (1979) Ecological Model (cited by Galpin, 2016).

ACTIVITY 4.1

Think about the meanings associated with the term 'loneliness' and 'social isolation'. How might these meanings relate to those that you work with? What factors contribute to their sense of loneliness?

How might an understanding of the individual within their wider ecological system be useful in understanding loneliness and social isolation?

In your experience how do different professional groups understand the impact of loneliness on an individual's physical and mental well-being?

Loneliness and well-being

As previously indicated, loneliness can affect an individual at any point in their lifecourse, and can lead to serious negative mental health consequences (Shevlin *et al.*, 2014). Loneliness and social isolation have been found to have serious detrimental impacts on both mental and physical health and well-being (Cacioppo *et al.*, 2014), and this can occur at any point in the lifecourse. For example, in a study of young people, loneliness and self-concept confusion have been linked to depression and have been found to undermine mental well-being (Joiner *et al.*, 2002). At the other end of the lifecourse, research with older people suggests that social isolation can increase feelings of loneliness, which in turn leads to deterioration in mental health status (Santini *et al.*, 2016). Feelings of loneliness may also signal the early signs of dementia (Holwerda *et al.*, 2012).

Feeling lonely therefore has a negative impact on mental well-being and it has been suggested that 'loneliness disrupts the clarity and structure of the self, which, in turn, disrupts people's mental health' (Richman *et al.*, 2016, p546). It is important to note that those with mental health conditions may be more susceptible to experiencing both loneliness and social isolation, as a result of their mental health status and the stigma attached to it. Other groups in society that experience social exclusion may be at increased risk of experiencing social isolation and loneliness, for example those from ethnic minority groups, those with disabilities or members of the LGBT community.

The use of stigmatising language and media portrayal of negative images about disability reinforce the marginalisation and oppression of many disabled people (Dupré, 2012). This in turn can leave those who are disabled at increased risk of experiencing social isolation and loneliness, and this may be exacerbated by physical barriers due to limited access to social spaces and reduced transport options. For example, older people with physical disabilities are at increased risk of experiencing depression (Bierman and Statland, 2010), and this may be linked to the functional limitations associated with their disability which prevent them accessing social relationships leading to less perceived social support (Taylor and Lynch, 2004).

Loneliness has also been found to undermine well-being for those with learning disabilities, who may face social exclusion and isolation (Al-Yagon and Margalit, 2013; Margalit, 2012). People with learning disabilities may be targeted by 'predatory groups and individuals who pretend to be friends but who are really taking advantage of people' (Gravell, 2012, p2). People who feel lonely may respond positively to any form of social contact, even when this occurs as part of a ploy to exploit them for financial gain. This desire for friendship and social contact may be exploited by scammers who 'befriend' the lonely individual.

The feeling of being lonely, which is linked to a lack of social engagement with others, and a lack of relatedness and belonging, not only undermines individual physical and mental well-being; it may also increase the likelihood of someone responding to a scam contact due to the opportunity for social connection it offers. People who feel lonely may therefore connect with other people without fully appraising the type of contact offered, or the strings attached to it. Some may even feel that a small cost attached to a financial scam is worth paying for as it provides much needed social contact. Scammers exploit this vulnerability and use lures and approaches which reinforce a 'relationship' with the victim which makes them feel special (Lea and Webley, 2006). Victims can therefore develop strong attachments to the person who is scamming them which is based on a social relationship which is reinforced over time and through multiple contacts.

ACTIVITY 4.2

Thinking about social contacts and loneliness

Think about a service user you work with.

1. Have they left their home during the past week?

2. Who have they spoken to during the past week?

   (a) in person

   (b) on the phone/mobile phone

   (c) online via webcam

3. Who have they written to or received mail from during the past week?

   (a) letters

   (b) texts

   (c) emails online

This activity will give you an idea of the types of social contacts a person has.

Loneliness and old age

It is important for practitioners who work with older people to recognise the risks to health and well-being that loneliness presents. Loneliness and the associated vulnerability it brings is a significant but under-recognised problem for older adults (Alves and Wilson, 2008). There are about 3.5 million people aged 65+ living alone in the UK (Age UK, 2016). Although living alone does not necessarily lead to loneliness, research by Age UK (2016) indicates that 200,000 older people (65 and over) have not had a conversation with friends or family for a month, and 12.04 per cent or 1.2 million older people (65 and over in England) are persistently/chronically lonely. Social isolation can mean older people are often without social support and integration, which are both positively related to health and well-being (Kang and Ridgway, 1996). Other social and cultural factors may increase the risk of older people feeling lonely, and research suggests that there is a direct correlation between low income, loneliness and social isolation among older people (Bolton, 2012). In particular, a lack of informal support has been found to have a serious impact on the health and well-being of low-income older women leading to loss of independence and premature institutionalisation (Ryser and Halseth, 2011).

Research suggests that there is a consistent correlation between a lack of social support and abuse of older people (Acierno *et al.*, 2010), whereas high levels of social support may reduce both the vulnerability of older people and their risk of abuse (Melchiorre *et al.*, 2013). Older people may have less opportunity to engage with social support as they are more vulnerable to problems of social isolation compared to younger cohorts due to limited mobility, decreasing social networks due to death of their partner(s) and peers, and changes in their social roles due to retirement and loss of income (Social Care Institute for Excellence, 2012). Feelings of loneliness can have negative mental and physical health consequences and research suggests that loneliness in later life can increase the risk of premature death by 30 per cent (Holt-Lunstad *et al.*, 2015).

It has been suggested that 'socially isolated older adults' are 'highly vulnerable to financial scams and manipulations' (Lubben *et al.*, 2015, p5), and financial scams targeting older people have been described as the crime of the twenty-first century (NCA, 2015). For some older people their only form of social contact comes from market-based communication such as telemarketing phone calls. Older people may be more trusting, and are therefore more likely to respond to the approaches made by scammers. This also makes them less likely to recognise when they are being scammed. Being more trusting of approaches which appear 'official' means that older people are not as aware of the dangers of giving out personal information, such as credit card and bank account numbers, over the phone.

Research suggests that strong relationships can form between socially isolated individuals and perpetrators of financial scams because of the quantity rather than quality of the contact (Kang and Ridgway, 1996). Numerous daily phone calls or a constant stream of scam mail may be perceived positively by the lonely older person who regards them as socially supportive in the absence of other types of relationship. The frequency of scam contact can become more highly valued than the actual quality of contact, and as a result the benefits of communication with a scammer outweigh the potential costs. Socially isolated older people are more likely to respond to telemarketing phone calls, doorstep sales and scam mail. They are more likely to listen to a sales pitch (Lee and Geistfeld, 1999), and as a result are more likely to be vulnerable to financial scams and manipulations (Lubben *et al.*, 2015). In particular older people who are feeling lonely at home may be at increased risk of being targeted by telephone fraud. A study in the US has found that the telephone was the most commonly used method of contact for older people targeted for consumer fraud (Holtfreter *et al.*, 2014).

Obviously alleviating the social isolation that older people experience is one way to help combat loneliness in old age, and this may have a positive impact on general well-being. Alongside this, purposeful social activity has been identified as an important aspect of well-being in later life (Allpass *et al.*, 2007), and this would appear to be congruent with the safeguarding principles of empowerment, partnership and protection (DH, 2013). This supports an approach which facilitates social engagement in community activity to promote older people's self-esteem (WHO, 2007). This in turn may build individual resilience in later life (Wild *et al.*, 2013), and can also be a useful consideration when considering the wider impact of the five inter-related domains of Bronfenbrenner's model (see Figure 4.1).

CASE STUDY 4.1

An older man lived in the community with his wife of 20 years. When she died suddenly he became socially isolated as there were no adult children and no extended family to support him. At this time he began engaging with competition mail. Initially it was a single letter purporting that he had won a lottery in Australia and needed to pay an advanced fee to release his winnings. The competition involved some puzzles to solve as well in order to qualify for a higher grade of winnings. Moreover it required him to pay increasingly large sums of money with increased frequency into the scammers' account. Several more 'wins' followed in different competitions.

The man came to the attention of authorities when his post office noticed that he was coming in more frequently than before and that he appeared to have lost weight. When the cashier questioned him he initially told her of what he believed was his good fortune before getting angry at her dismissal of the letters as fraudulent. Due to their concern post office staff contacted the council and the matter was taken as a safeguarding one. However the man declined to let social workers in. It was only when the social workers asked a trading standards officer to accompany them that he engaged, initially only at the doorstep. After three doorstep conversations over about ten days, the client allowed trading standards and social workers into the property. The scale of the issue became apparent as he had little food in the house.

It came to light that he was spending all of his private and state pension on the scams as he was convinced that he was about to win large sums of money from each one. He was playing in the region of 20 competitions, all of which required him to send off varying amounts of 'release fees'. Moreover the phone rang consistently as the scammers had morphed their scam from simple competition mail to phone calls (after asking for his phone number on one of the response papers). As such they now contacted him and were fishing for information about his house and other fixed assets. When asked why he had engaged he replied that the competition mail had taken his mind off the loss of his wife and that it had given him something to do as he had 'a lot of paper work' and the requirement to go to the post office several times a week gave him a 'reason to leave the house'. Furthermore he enjoyed the phone calls as the men were largely friendly and even sympathetic with him over the death of his wife and he found this comforting.

The man was assisted with a call blocking system on his phone to stop the harassment and helped with daily bank limits to prevent catastrophic fraud taking place. Despite having full

(Continued)

CASE STUDY 4.1 (CONT.)

mental capacity he remained only partially convinced by the argument made by social work-
ers and trading standards that the competitions were a scam. As such he continued to enter
but agreed to a £10 weekly limit. He was assisted ongoing by a financial advocate from the
third sector to help him monitor his finances.

Sean Olivier, Safeguarding Adults Coordinator
for the London Borough of Croydon and Trish Burls,
Principal Trading Standards Officer for London Borough of Croydon

---

ACTIVITY 4.3

Thinking about the above case study, how might an understanding of the individual using
Bronfenbrenner's (1979) Ecological Model (cited by Galpin, 2016) be useful in under-
standing some of the factors which may have contributed to his scam involvement? What
might some of these factors be?

When considering the impact of loneliness on well-being, it is import to understand
the person in context, for example in relation to age, physical or mental status, cognitive ability etc.

The Missing Million Guide (2016) offers some useful prompts when considering
triggers for loneliness.

- What does their social world look like to them, and how is it experienced?

- Does the person have supportive relationships with family and friends?

- Are there local formal or informal social groups to which the person belongs or could
  belong?

- Are there factors that prevent social connection, such as a lack of transport?

- Has the person experienced a recent significant change in their life (this might include
  bereavement, moving house, retiring, physical ill health, stopping driving)?

(Campaign to End Loneliness, 2016, p16)

Combating loneliness and financial scam involvement

As the discussion in this chapter has indicated, loneliness and social isolation are inter-
related concepts, and can both undermine health and well-being. Feeling lonely can

make an individual more likely to respond to a scam contact, particularly if it is the only contact with another person they have had that day, or week, or month. People who are socially isolated are at increased risk of responding to scams, not only because they welcome new social contacts, but also because they have fewer opportunities to meet with others to discuss finances or scams (Age UK, 2015). They are therefore unable to 'check out' with anyone else if an approach is genuine or part of a scam. Socially isolated people can also be less familiar with normal business practices and as a result are more vulnerable to missing the cues of a scam (Lee and Geistfeld, 1999).

The Doorstep Crime Victim Impact Survey (2015) found that 57 per cent of the people who reported doorstep scams lived alone, 41 per cent felt lonely and 34 per cent had experienced recent bereavement (National Trading Standards Board, 2015). Certain types of scams are particularly targeted on lonely people. For example, romance scams exploit an individual's desire for a meaningful relationship, and make their victim believe that they have a strong emotional bond and relationship based on love. The romantic component of the scam acts as a bait to lure victims, before committing other types of fraud, such as identity theft and financial fraud (Arms, 2010). This can be particularly emotionally devastating for the victim (Whitty and Buchanan, 2012a).

It is important that agencies respond in a supportive way to victims of scams to prevent further social isolation occurring, particularly as victims can often be reluctant to report the scam in the first place. A 'victim-blaming discourse' is a significant factor in isolating victims and negatively influencing their ability to disclose to those around them (Cross, 2015, p187). If individuals are depicted as 'foolish' due to their scam involvement, they are likely to be blamed for their losses rather than seen as a victim in need of support.

Loneliness is a multi-faceted issue and may not be simply resolved by tackling one aspect alone. Similar to adult safeguarding responses, it requires a multi-agency approach which is founded upon clear communication and partnership working. Agencies could use 'well-being' as a common theme around which care and support is developed to tackle both loneliness and promote adult safeguarding (Care Act 2014; Guidance, 2016). Building on the work of Cattan *et al.* (2005), a number of broad characteristics should underpin good loneliness intervention:

- Adopt a person-centred approach – explore with the individual their interests, the type of experience they are facing: isolation or loneliness.

- In line with Making Safeguarding Personal guidance (LGA, 2014) involve each person in developing a plan to promote their own well-being, and this might include consideration of their social well-being and connections within the wider community.

- Community development initiatives can build resilience for individuals and communities to combat loneliness (Nicholl, 2014). This builds upon a community assets approach.

- Explore opportunities which empower the individual to safeguard themselves against scam involvement. For example, setting up groups to promote financial awareness and literacy, and accessing learning materials through 'Friends Against Scams' and 'Scamsmart' (FCA, 2014) initiatives.

- Promote opportunities of inter-professional learning and joint working across agencies to promote the well-being of lonely people at risk of scam involvement to support more 'joined up' interventions.

- At a more strategic level, explore option of addressing loneliness as an outcome measure of council strategies which include the Joint Strategic Needs Assessment (JSNA) and the Joint Health and Wellbeing Strategy (JHWS) (LGA, 2016c). This could also include joint working with Safeguarding Adults Boards to create more joined up approaches to well-being, loneliness and adult safeguarding.

Key learning points

- Loneliness is a subjective experience and relates to the individual's perception of their social connections.

- Social isolation is a descriptive term and relates to a lack of social contact or an absence of social connections within the wider community.

- Loneliness can undermine an individual's health and well-being, and can increase vulnerability to responding to a scam.

- Individual vulnerability to loneliness can increase in response to specific life events such as bereavement, chronic illness, ageing and social isolation.

- Socially isolated and lonely people are at increased risk of responding to scams, not only because they welcome new social contacts, but because they have fewer opportunities to check out the nature of a scam contact with others.

- Some fraudsters and scammers manipulate their contact with lonely isolated individuals by 'befriending' them, and by maintaining high levels of contact with them over a period of time to build a 'trusting' relationship with their victims.

- As loneliness undermines well-being, agencies could use 'well-being' as a common theme around which care and support is developed to tackle loneliness whilst promoting adult safeguarding around financial scams.

OTHER RESOURCES

Campaign to end loneliness.

http://www.campaigntoendloneliness.org.uk/

The Joseph Rowntree Loneliness Resource Pack.

https://www.jrf.org.uk/report/loneliness-resource-pack

SCIE research briefing 39: Preventing loneliness and social isolation: interventions and outcomes.

http://www.scie.org.uk/publications/briefings/briefing39/

The Missing Million: A practical guide to identifying and talking about loneliness 2016.

http://www.campaigntoendloneliness.org/wp-content/uploads/CEL-Missing-Millions-Guide_final.pdf

Chapter 5

Dementia, safeguarding and scam involvement

Lee-Ann Fenge

CHAPTER OUTCOMES

As a result of completing this chapter you will:

- Understand what dementia is and its impact on the individual.

- Understand the impact of dementia on well-being and how it may be an important consideration in terms of promoting well-being as defined by the Care Act.

- Understand what dementia might mean within safeguarding and Making Safeguarding Personal.

- Understand how dementia may lead some individuals to be at increased risk of becoming involved in financial scams.

Introduction

This chapter sets out to consider how knowledge and understanding of the impact of dementia is important for those involved in adult safeguarding activity. In particular it considers how dementia may make individuals vulnerable to financial abuse and financial scams. This is an important topic to explore as dementia is a condition which is growing in prevalence: it is suggested that there are currently 850,000 people with dementia in the UK (Prince *et al.*, 2014), and by 2051 this is projected to rise to over two million people (Kane and Terry, 2015). As the worldwide population gets older, so the number of those with dementia increases, and it is estimated that globally the number of those with dementia will surpass 135 million by 2050 (Alzheimer's Disease International, 2013).

Health and social care practitioners are increasingly coming into contact with service users and patients who have dementia and whose well-being is compromised by the condition. For example, it is estimated that a quarter of hospital beds are now occupied by people with dementia (Alzheimer's Society, 2009). It is important that all public services consider the impact of dementia on safeguarding adults activity and how the condition may increase vulnerability to financial abuse and financial scams. The future well-being and care choices available to individuals with dementia may be restricted if they lose their savings to financial exploitation and scams. This issue has growing relevance as individuals are increasingly expected to contribute to their care costs in later life and as Rabiner *et al.* (2005, p53) suggest, 'Financial exploitation may deprive victims of their life savings and assets and, thus, their economic foundation for independence.'

As highlighted in previous chapters, practitioners in the public sector need knowledge and understanding of the duties that agencies now have as a result of the Care Act 2014 to safeguard individuals from financial abuse. In particular they need awareness of how dementia may increase individual vulnerability to responding to scam contacts. For example, cognitive impairment due to dementia creates vulnerability because of its negative effect on financial capacity, decision-making capacity, and judgement linked to finances (Choi *et al.*, 1999; Marson *et al.*, 2009). This may make the individual less able to distinguish between a genuine financial contact and a scam contact, and also less able to make judgements linked to the value of money. For example, if a doorstep rogue trader offers to mow the lawn for £500, the inflated cost of this service may lack meaning for the individual lacking financial capacity due to dementia, and they may hand over £500 for a service which takes 10 minutes to complete.

The need to increase awareness and understanding of financial abuse and its implications for dementia and adult safeguarding has been acknowledged in *A Curriculum for UK Dementia Education*. This highlights how important it is to 'identify abusive or exploitative practice and take action to prevent its occurrence' (HEDN, 2014, p52). General society is becoming more aware of the experiences of those with dementia and their carers through recent policy which has emphasised the need for inclusive and responsive provision (Alzheimer's Society, 2013a; DH, 2016b). For example, in the UK *Challenge on Dementia 2020* aims to create 4 million dementia friends by 2020, and at least 100 more dementia friendly communities (DH, 2016b). This reflects an approach to dementia which has at its heart a commitment to promote a dementia friendly society globally (WHO, 2012). As well as supporting a human rights approach to dementia, it also emphasises the importance of maintaining links with local networks as 'it is generally beneficial for people with dementia to have the stability of remaining in the familiar surroundings of their own homes and local neighbourhoods' (Mitchell *et al.*, 2004, p90).

In the UK, two-thirds of people with dementia live in the community while one-third live in a care home (Alzheimer's Society, 2014). It is positive that individuals can remain living in their communities for longer, and it is important that agencies providing support to them are alert to the ways in which they may be targeted by doorstep rogue traders, and by mail, telephone and internet scammers. To begin with, the chapter will explore what dementia is, and considers the implications of dementia on safeguarding adults at risk of harm activity. The chapter will then consider how dementia might increase an individual's vulnerability to scam involvement.

What is dementia?

Dementia is an umbrella term and represents a group of conditions associated with an ongoing decline of brain function and its abilities. Dementia affects memory, thinking, language, understanding and judgement, and can have a devastating impact on well-being, increasing levels of disability and dependency in those that experience it. According to the World Health Organization (2016) globally there are 47.5 million people with dementia and there are 7.7 million new cases every year.

There are different types of dementia which have different causes, but all of them will impact upon cognitive function.

Main types of dementia

Alzheimer's disease – *the most common cause of dementia. It is a progressive condition resulting from the build-up of proteins in the brain which form structures called 'plaques' and 'tangles'. This leads to the loss of connections between nerve cells, and eventually the loss of brain tissue.*

Vascular dementia – *this is related to reduced blood supply to the brain as a result of diseased blood vessels. There are different types of vascular dementia, and some are linked to the experience of strokes (for example, multi-infarct dementia is caused by one or more smaller strokes). Alongside cognitive decline, individuals with early vascular dementia may experience mood changes, such as apathy, depression or anxiety as they become aware of the changes in their brain function.*

Dementia with Lewy bodies – *this type of dementia is a progressive condition and shares symptoms with both Alzheimer's disease and Parkinson's disease, and accounts for 10–15 per cent of all cases of dementia. Lewy bodies are tiny deposits of a protein (alpha-synuclein) that appear in nerve cells. People with a Lewy body disorder can have problems with movement and changes in mental abilities at the same time. Visual hallucinations are also a common feature of this type of dementia.*

Frontotemporal dementia (FTD) or Pick's disease – *one of the less common types of dementia which covers a wide range of different conditions. It is sometimes called Pick's disease or frontal lobe dementia and can lead to changes in personality and behaviour, as well as difficulties with language. These symptoms are different from the memory loss often associated with more common types of dementia, such as Alzheimer's disease.*

*(Based on Types of Dementia Factsheets produced by the Alzheimer's Society, available from **https://www.alzheimers.org.uk/typesofdementia**)*

It is important that professionals remain alert to these signs as the early stages of dementia are often overlooked as the onset is gradual. At least half of those with dementia do not receive a diagnosis (Alzheimer's Society, 2014), and this means that many people with dementia and their carers are living in the community without the support or recognition they need.

Signs of dementia

Early stage: Onset is gradual and early symptoms may include:

- *forgetfulness*
- *losing track of the time*
- *becoming lost in familiar places.*

Middle stage: As dementia progresses the signs and symptoms become more obvious and include:

- *becoming forgetful of recent events and people's names*
- *becoming lost at home*
- *increasing difficulty with communication*
- *needing help with personal care*
- *behaviour changes, including wandering and repeated questioning.*

Late stage: The late stage of dementia is one of near total dependence and inactivity; symptoms include:

- *being unaware of the time and place*
- *difficulty recognising relatives and friends*
- *increasing need for assisted self-care*
- *difficulty walking*
- *behaviour changes that may escalate and include aggression.*

(Based on WHO (2016) Dementia Factsheet)

Professionals need to develop a balanced understanding of what dementia may mean for individuals and their families. Negative representations of dementia tend to reinforce stigma as it is portrayed as one of the most dreaded set of symptoms in contemporary society (Van Gorp and Vercruyesse, 2012). Dementia is depicted as silently overwhelming health and social care resources with terms such as 'silent tsunami' and 'wave of dementia' (Zeiling, 2013). Such negative images can have a detrimental impact on those that have dementia as we derive pictures of ourselves through how others view us, and this in turn impacts on how we view ourselves.

The adverse images associated with dementia have been identified as a major barrier preventing individuals seeking treatment and support (Alzheimer's Society, 2008). An approach which focuses on loss and deficits can lead society to wholly underestimate the abilities of those with the symptoms, and expect less of them as a result. This in turn can prompt decreases in self-esteem, mental, social and physical well-being and increase the risk of depression (Smith, 2010). It is therefore important to focus on the assets the individual has by adopting a person-centred approach which is focused on enhancing well-being rather than just focusing on deficits. This relates to the concept of 'personhood' (SCIE, 2013), and 'It is important to understand how people with dementia see themselves and their surroundings because this can influence how they manage their condition' (SCIE, 2013, p2). This may be particularly important when supporting individuals to enhance their financial capability and awareness of the risks posed by financial scams.

ACTIVITY **5.1**

Think about the meanings associated with the term 'dementia'. How might these meanings relate to those that you work with? How might the language used to describe dementia contribute to the isolation that individuals experience as a result of a dementia diagnosis?

In your experience how do different professional groups understand the impact of dementia on an individual's physical and mental well-being?

Dementia friendly communities and social inclusion

In recent years the policy emphasis in dementia care has been on inclusion and the development of 'dementia friendly' communities and services (Alzheimer's Society, 2013a). This includes initiatives to include people living with dementia in daily life and also education and awareness-raising of dementia within the general population. A key element of inclusive dementia friendly communities is a focus on improved communication skills for those providing services and provision to those with dementia (Alzheimer's Society, 2013b). However, it is important to acknowledge that there is the potential for 'dementia friendly communities' and the language around them to become stigmatising for those with dementia as it can reinforce an 'us and them' culture (Swaffer, 2014). It is therefore important that such approaches resonate with a commitment to value those with dementia and engage with their views and experiences. This approach is reinforced by a World Health Organization report (2012) which stresses the importance of including people with dementia, their caregivers and families to improve understanding of dementia and reduce the stigma associated with it.

Dementia friendly communities have in themselves been questioned as a way of colluding with the wider societal structures which serve to reinforce marginalisation and oppression. Rather than a homogenised view of dementia, Wright (2014) argues for an approach which acknowledges the social, cultural, political and economic inter-sections which lead to discrimination and marginalisation within the lived experience of dementia, resulting in increased disadvantage and marginalisation for certain groups linked to gender, ethnicity and poverty. For example, cultural differences in understanding what dementia is may result in a lack of appropriate support. A research briefing by SCIE (2011b) indicates that there is no word for dementia in most South Asian languages and lower levels of awareness in Black Caribbean and Irish communities. As a result people from BME communities are more likely to see the symptoms of dementia as part of normal ageing rather than as a result of physiological changes in the brain.

REFLECTION **5.1**

When considering the impact of dementia on well-being it is important to understand the person in context, for example in relation to age, physical or mental status, cognitive abil-ity etc. Think of an individual with dementia you have worked with and consider how their specific context influences their experience of dementia and its impact on their well-being. This may include social, cultural, political and economic considerations.

A dementia friendly approach is 'one in which people with dementia are empowered to have high aspirations and feel confident, knowing they can contribute and partici-pate in activities that are meaningful to them' (Alzheimer's Society, 2013a, pviii). It is also important for practitioners to recognise the marginalisation and social exclusion experienced by carers of those with dementia. Daly *et al.* (2013, p501) describes how the stigma of living with and caring for someone who has dementia can result in 'living on the fringes'. Organisations need to support social inclusion and social con-nectedness within familiar settings and community provision for individuals as well as their families.

Dementia and financial capability

Dementia is progressive and the condition changes a person's abilities over time, including fluctuating capacity to make decisions and judge risk in everyday circum-stances (Alzheimer's Society, 2014). In a survey concerning money management, 76 per cent of people with dementia reported that they had experienced difficulties in managing their finances (Alzheimer's Society, 2011). Those with dementia may not have the financial capacity skills to judge risk and can find it more difficult to apply precautionary measures to decision-making, which puts them at increased risk of responding to a scam. As a consequence there is a relationship between financial capacity and financial exploitation, as the potential loss of financial skills and financial decision-making has a negative impact upon the ability to detect and prevent finan-cial exploitation (Stiegel, 2012). However, this is a little explored area and there is currently a dearth of research exploring financial capacity for those with dementia (Boyle, 2013). Although financial matters are central to the experience of well-being for service users and carers, and many social work practitioners deal with financially vulnerable people on a daily basis (Fenge, 2011), student social workers receive little financial literacy education (Sherraden *et al.*, 2007).

It is vital that all professionals coming into contact with individuals with dementia remain mindful of the impact of dementia on the individual's financial capability and vulnerability to financial abuse and financial scams. Those with dementia may be specifically targeted by those who wish to exploit them financially as it can be more difficult to detect scams and financial abuse in people who have dementia because of a lack of confidence in their credibility (Alzheimer's Society, 2011). Approaches by scammers which might include a barrage of phone calls or mail contact may be particularly upsetting for someone who has dementia. In a study by the Alzheimer's Society (2011), 70 per cent of carers said that the person they cared for had been targeted by cold callers via the telephone and 40 per cent had been targeted by scam mail. New technology, the rise of phone and internet banking alongside the closure of many bank branches may create added challenges to financial management for those with dementia.

It is important that practitioners remain alert to the ways in which dementia can make a person an 'easy target' for financial scams and abuse. Depending on the stage of dementia, the person may not have the financial capacity to understand what they are being asked for, or how to respond to a scam which is being targeted at them. They may also not have the ability to remember what has happened to them, or the ability to remember that they responded to a similar scam the week before. Even when a person with dementia does disclose abuse they may not be believed, or they may not be seen as a credible or reliable witness.

Social and demographic changes influencing the issue of financial management for people with dementia

- *Rapid changes in the way people manage their finances. For example, online transactions, cash machines, telephone banking and declining use of cheques. This could make it more difficult for people with dementia to manage their own finances, and leave them more open to financial scams.*

- *The number of people with dementia who have pensions, property and other resources may attract those keen to exploit them through fraud and theft.*

- *Financial decision-making also presents wider concerns for people with dementia, including questions about inheritance, inter-generational relationships and debates about paying and charging for care.*

(Based on 'Short changed: Protecting people with dementia from financial abuse' (Alzheimer's Society, 2011, p15))

Victims of financial scams often find it hard to talk about their experiences and an individual with dementia may be experiencing even more distress because they already have difficulties in communicating their experiences. Clear and effective communication with those with dementia and their families is vital to increase their awareness of potential financial scams. Good communication also involves active listening, and providing the space and opportunities for the individual to share their experiences in their own words.

Communication is a key element for the development of dementia friendly environments to create a sense of belonging and to preserve a sense of identity for the person with dementia (Alzheimer's Society, 2013c). Caring for people with dementia requires specific communication skills to support meaningful interactions (Eggenberger *et al.*, 2013). An essential element of good communication is well-developed listening skills which support person-centred interaction. This should be focused on the use of accessible language and an awareness of environment to minimise noise and distraction (Livability, 2016). Communication is not just linked to verbal communication, but also involves making use of non-verbal communication, and this may become more important if the person has limited speech (Allan, 2001). Communication training, such as the Communication Enhancement Model (Ryan *et al.*, 1995), has been shown to have a positive impact on the quality of person-centred communication which empowers those with dementia (Sprangers *et al.*, 2015), and 'Making Safeguarding Personal' should be informed by a commitment to good communication and partnership working.

Communications skills and dementia

- *Speak clearly and slowly, using short sentences.*
- *Make eye contact with the person when they're talking.*
- *Allow time for the individual to respond.*
- *Encourage them to join in conversations with others.*
- *Encourage them to speak for themselves.*
- *Acknowledge what they have said, even if they don't answer your question, or what they say seems out of context – show that you've heard them and encourage them to say more about their answer.*
- *Give individuals simple choices – avoid creating complicated choices.*
- *Explore other ways to communicate – such as rephrasing questions because they can't answer in the way they used to.*

(Based on: NHS Guide 'Communicating with people with dementia',
*available from: **http://www.nhs.uk/Conditions/dementia-guide/***
***Pages/dementia-and-communication.aspx**)*

An approach which tries to actively tune into the experiences of people with dementia as they are experiencing them in the 'here and now' has been described as 'empathic curiosity' (McEvoy and Plant, 2014). This requires the practitioners to engage in empathic listening and to maintain a curious attitude (particularly in regard to non-verbal cues and behaviours). In terms of involvement in financial scams, this might mean using an approach to communication which helps create a space in which the person can talk about their current experiences, using open questions in the present tense, which allow the practitioner to pick up on the emotional cues within the conversation. McEvoy *et al.* (2014, p13) suggest that 'when someone pauses, falters, looks away, shakes their head or laughs to themselves, these disruptions may indicate that they are distracted by their background thoughts'. These types of non-verbal communication provide opportunities to ask people with dementia about their thoughts, and they may then start talking about concerns or issues that are on their mind (Carey, 2008, cited in McEvoy *et al.*, 2014).

Safeguarding, well-being and dementia

In terms of Making Safeguarding Personal guidance (Lawson *et al.*, 2014), it is important to consider how practitioners work with the individual with dementia in a manner which is cognisant of the six safeguarding principles outlined by the Department of Health (DH, 2013). As highlighted in previous chapters these include:

- Empowerment
- Partnership
- Protection
- Prevention
- Proportionality
- Accountability.

Interventions should aim to empower individuals within safeguarding contexts to remain safe from potential financial exploitation. For example, in Scotland funding is being given to a project which aims to empower residents with dementia to live safely and independently in their own homes without being bombarded with confusing and intimidating calls or unsolicited doorstep cold callers (Life Changes Trust, 2016). Three Scottish local authorities (East Renfrewshire, Angus and South Ayrshire) are working together to develop a preventative approach to protect people with dementia from financial exploitation. The approach includes practical solutions and various types of useful technology such as call blockers which screen incoming phone calls. Funding for the project has come from the Life Changes Trust, an independent charity set up with a Big Lottery Fund endowment of £50 million (for further details see **http://www.lifechangestrust.org.uk**).

In all safeguarding activity due regard must be given to the Mental Capacity Act 2005 (MCA). When considering safeguarding for individuals with dementia it is essential that supported decision-making is focused on the outcomes the person wishes to achieve, including consideration of what is working in their lives and what is not. There should be a mechanism to clearly guide and record the 'conversation' about choice and risk. A balance sheet approach may be helpful in looking at the risks and benefits of any decision. It is important to recognise that current financial systems may hinder safeguarding activity, and professionals may perceive bank procedures and rules as significant barriers towards safeguarding vulnerable adults from financial abuse (Alzheimer's Society, 2011, pviii). In part this may be related to a lack of understanding of dementia and mental capacity by bank officials, or an appreciation of the impact this may have on the ability to manage finances. Staff in banks and other financial institutions, who come into contact with members of the public, should have a working understanding of advance decisions and Lasting Power of Attorney (LPA) which are enshrined in the Mental Capacity Act 2005.

In England and Wales, the Mental Capacity Act 2005 (MCA) provides a much needed framework for making decisions and for setting out a person's wishes about what they wish to happen if their ability to make decisions is impaired. Please see Chapter 6 which provides an in-depth discussion of mental capacity and the MCA 2005. The Act assumes that all individuals have the capacity to make decisions for themselves unless otherwise determined. The act has three broad objectives:

1. To support people with impaired capacity so that they can make decisions for themselves.

2. Where they cannot take a particular decision for themselves, to provide them with a protective framework for decisions that are made about them.

3. To provide a framework for those who have to make and implement decisions in relation to people who do not have the capacity to make those decisions for themselves.

There are two types of Lasting Power of Attorney (LPA), one for property and finances, and one for health and welfare. If a person lacks capacity to make a decision and have not made an LPA or advance decision, it may be necessary to apply to the Court of Protection to make the decision in the person's best interests.

CASE STUDY 5.1

A man in his late sixties had been enjoying his retirement for 8 years. He had previously worked in an office environment for 35 years. He lived in his own house and managed, for the most part, independently. He had a nephew who visited roughly once a week to help his uncle with home maintenance and shopping.

The nephew noted that his uncle had begun collecting an odd collection of items in his front room. His uncle had said that they were free gifts and prizes from a competition.

In further visits the collection of gifts grew, but these were items his uncle had never expressed an interest in and he did not seem to use them (such as salad bowls and ornaments). The nephew also noticed that his uncle had increasing post and that his front room was cluttered with papers where it had not been before.

A friend from the church referred the adult to the local trading standards team as they had been concerned that it was a scam. Trading standards officers went to visit and felt that the client was engaging with competition mail. They also had concerns for the client's ability to understand their argument that the post was a scam. He also appeared to not remember the salient features of their discussion from earlier in the visit.

A social worker was allocated and went to visit the client with the same trading standards officer. The social worker shared the concerns about the client's understanding of the scam and risk posed to his finances. The client was still reluctant to share the full details of his engagement and so the risk to his finances was difficult to gauge. The social worker assessed that the client lacked capacity to understand the risk associated with engaging with competition mail. A referral to the GP was made to consider if there were any physical health factors.

While attempting to set up a best interest meeting with the GP and the nephew the client was admitted to hospital with a UTI. As such the ward psychiatrist repeated the mental capacity assessment shortly before the client was discharged when his infection had abated. Again it was felt that the adult lacked capacity to understand the risks posed by engaging with the scam mail.

A best interest meeting was set up shortly after his discharge. In the interim the client had continued to send money to scammers and effectively turned his front room into an office and operated largely as though he was back in his job. He was also diagnosed with dementia. The client appeared to believe that his scam mail and associated paper work was his job and eagerly awaited the post arrival each day, sitting by the door in anticipation of the deliveries. The gifts received appeared to reciprocate his frequent small sums of money sent off and validated, in his mind, his spend (which far exceeded the value of the gifts).

Following the best interest meeting the nephew approached the Court of Protection for Guardianship which was granted and comprehensive financial protection planning could take place, as well as paying off of debts that had been incurred. A mail redirection was also put on to prevent scam mail reaching the client's front door.

Sean Olivier, Safeguarding Adults Coordinator
for the London Borough of Croydon and Trish Burls,
Principal Trading Standards Officer for London Borough of Croydon

ACTIVITY 5.2

Thinking about the above case study how might an understanding of dementia and mental capacity be useful in understanding some of the factors which may have contributed to his scam involvement? What might some of these factors be?

It is helpful for all practitioners working with those who have dementia in adult safeguarding contexts to develop understanding of issues related to financial capacity and financial decision-making. This might include supporting carers in making sense of the Mental Capacity Act 2005 which both confirms and extends the rights of people to appoint proxy decision-makers. This also relates to the legal principles which underpin best interests decision-making (see Code of Practice, Office of the Public Guardian, 2007). Agencies should ensure that staff are equipped with information about finances and financial capacity which can be shared with people with dementia and their families if required.

Key learning points

- Dementia is a condition which we are becoming more aware of, together with the needs and experiences of those with the disorder.

- Dementia can undermine an individual's health and well-being, and can increase vulnerability to responding to a scam.

- There is a relationship between financial capacity and financial exploitation, as the potential loss of financial skills and financial decision-making has a negative impact upon the ability to detect and prevent financial exploitation.

- The approaches used by some scammers, which include bombarding the individual with either phone or mail contact, can be particularly distressing for someone who has dementia.

- Some fraudsters and scammers manipulate their contact with people with dementia by exploiting their cognitive deficits to increase the likelihood of the individual responding to a scam.

- By adhering to the principles within Making Safeguarding Personal (MSP), agencies can promote 'well-being' as a common theme around which care and support is developed, empowering individuals and promoting understanding about financial scams.

- It is important that active listening and enhanced communication skills underpin practice with individuals with dementia.

- The Mental Capacity Act 2005 (MCA) provides a useful framework for making decisions and for setting out a person's wishes about what they want to happen if their ability to make decisions is impaired.

- Professionals need to develop a working understanding of the MCA 2005, and of the use of Lasting Power of Attorney (LPA).

- In some circumstances it may be necessary to apply to the Court of Protection to make the decision in the person's best interests in terms of their financial protection.

Alzheimer's Society (2014) Local dementia prevalence data by local authority, clinical commissioning group and parliamentary constituency. Available from: https://www.alzheimers.org.uk/site/scripts/download_info.php?fileID=2496

Alzheimer's Society (2015) Dementia 2015: Aiming higher to transform lives. Available from: https://www.alzheimers.org.uk/site/scripts/download_info.php?downloadID=1677

Alzheimer's Society (2016) Fact Sheet Communication. Available from: https://www.alzheimers.org.uk/site/scripts/download_info.php?downloadID=1128

Care UK (2014) Listen, talk, connect: Communicating with people living with dementia. Available from: http://www.careuk.com/sites/default/files/CareUK_Dementia_Guide.pdf

NHS (2015) Communicating with people with dementia. Available from: http://www.nhs.uk/Conditions/dementia-guide/Pages/dementia-and-communication.aspx

Social Care Institute for Excellence (SCIE) (2013) Dementia gateway: Making decisions. Available from: http://www.scie.org.uk/dementia/supporting-people-with-dementia/decisions/files/making-decisions.pdf

Chapter 6

Mental capacity, safeguarding and considering best interests

Mike Lyne

CHAPTER OUTCOMES

As a result of completing this chapter you will:

- Understand what mental capacity is and its impact on the individual.

- Understand the impact of mental capacity and the legislation underpinning it including the Mental Capacity Act 2005 (the Act or MCA).

- Understand the impact of mental capacity within adult safeguarding and Making Safeguarding Personal.

- Understand how issues linked to mental capacity may lead some individuals to be at increased risk of becoming involved in financial scams.

Anyone who meets and deals with other people either in the course of their professional or private lives may encounter issues of capacity. In effect, this means all of us. It is important to have some knowledge of mental capacity, the primary law which deals with this area and how to approach and deal with people whose abilities may be in question. Understanding mental capacity is especially relevant when working with victims of scams. The individual's ability to manage all, some or none of their financial affairs relates to their consequent potential vulnerability to financial exploitation.

The primary legislation in England and Wales dealing with this area of practice is the Mental Capacity Act 2005 (the Act or MCA) and this chapter will concentrate on the provisions of the Act in general terms and then on assessment of capacity and decision-making in more detail. However, it must be acknowledged that no law exists in isolation and, as such, the Act has links to and interfaces with, amongst others, the Care Act 2014, the European Convention on Human Rights and the Mental Health Act 1983, references to which may be found elsewhere in this text.

It is hoped that this chapter will provide information about the main provisions in this area of practice and provide a useful backdrop to Chapter 5. Further reading can be found in the references and bibliography.

For the purposes of this chapter, anyone deemed or suspected to lack capacity will be referred to as 'P'.

What is capacity?

Paragraph 4.1 of the Mental Capacity Act Code of Practice states that 'mental capacity is the ability to make a decision' (2007, p41). The Code separates decisions into two main categories: 'a decision that affects daily life such as when to get up, what to wear ...' or 'a decision that may have legal consequences for them or others. Examples include agreeing to have medical treatment, buying goods ...' (ibid).

This is a definition which is generally accepted by many different bodies including the Alzheimer's Society, the Mental Health Alliance, the College of Policing and others. And yet this has not always been the case. For instance, Tan and MacMillan (2004) pointed out that at that time, there was a difference between the legal and medical definitions and suggested that 'differences in guidance from various organisations is preventing uniform standards of practice' (p427).

The Law Society had commenced a project in 1989 to try and resolve some of these difficulties and to try and clarify the common law which was at the root of many of the issues. Based primarily on the principles of personal autonomy, 16 years after the commencement of the project, the MCA received Royal Assent in 2005, coming into force across England and Wales in 2007. The accompanying Code of Practice was published in 2007. The Act generally applies to those aged 16 or over although some provisions only come into play once 'P' has reached the age of 18. These particular provisions will be pointed out in the text.

Part 1: Main provisions of the Act

Five statutory principles

The Act is founded upon five statutory principles set out in section 1 of the Act:

1(2) A person must be assumed to have capacity unless it is established that he lacks capacity.

1(3) A person is not to be treated as unable to make a decision unless all practicable steps to help him to do so have been taken without success.

1(4) A person is not to be treated as unable to make a decision merely because he makes an unwise decision.

1(5) An act done, or a decision made, under this Act for or on behalf of a person who lacks capacity must be done, or made, in his best interests.

1(6) Before the act is done, or the decision is made, regard must be had to whether the purpose for which it is needed can be as effectively achieved in a way that is less restrictive of the person's rights and freedom of action.

(MCA 2005, s1)

The first and perhaps most fundamental principle is the idea that everyone can make their own decisions unless it is proven otherwise. This is known as the 'presumption of capacity' and is set out in section 1, subsection 2 of the Act. This will be explored further below.

Section 1(3) places the person who needs to make the decision ('P') at the centre of the process and attempts to remove previous paternalistic methods of making decisions by other people. 'All practicable steps' will include actions such as engaging the services of an interpreter for those people where English is a second language, but also include actions such as paying attention to the environment a decision is being made in, providing alternative methods of communication such as 'talking mats', etc.

Section 1(4) enforces the idea that people have the right to make 'unwise decisions' without that calling 'P's' decision-making abilities into question. This can be a difficult concept to work with as it can sometimes become enmeshed in risk taking. Responding to a scam, or continuing involvement in a scam, can be considered an 'unwise decision' which raises practice dilemmas.

The concept of making decisions in 'P's' best interests (1(5)) is not a new idea. Certainly, health and social care services have used this approach for many years. What the Act does is place this idea upon a formal footing and provide guidance in the form of a checklist as to what to take into account when making a decision for someone who is not able to make it themselves. An area of possible difficulty here is 'best interests' as this may also be used as a general societal phrase when acting on behalf of someone else, rather than the meaning enshrined within the MCA.

The final principle (1(6)) stresses the need to ensure that if one does have to take a decision on behalf of someone who cannot make it themselves, then it is essential to consider the restrictiveness of that decision and to try and lessen any overly burdensome or restrictive impact on the person. An area of difficulty here, especially for health and social care workers, may be the decision to place someone in residential care as opposed to living at home, as being at home is not always less restrictive than being in a care facility.

It does need to be remembered, though, that these principles are binding statements of law and are 'must do's'.

CASE STUDY 6.1, PART 1

Mrs Jones is a 75-year-old woman who lives alone in her own home. She has two daughters and a son. One of the daughters lives in Australia, but the other son and daughter live close by and visit their mother regularly. Other family members include Mrs Jones' brother, and three grandchildren all aged under 16.

Recently Mrs Jones has started to become forgetful. On one occasion Mrs Jones' son was called by a neighbour who reported that Mrs Jones had returned from shopping, but didn't appear to be able to find the right house. Mrs Jones' son attended and assisted his mother into her home. He found her to be distressed and tearful and he noticed that she had been incontinent. What steps should be taken in this situation?

Assessment of capacity and making best interest decisions

Prior to the onset of the Act there was no single test for deciding whether someone, possibly suffering from a cognitive issue, could make their own decisions. The MCA mostly resolves this with a two stage, so-called 'diagnostic' and 'functional' test for capacity (ss 2 and 3).

Where an inability to make a decision is proven, the Act sets out the process by which any such decisions should be made (s4). Both the assessment of capacity and the process of best interests decision-making will be discussed in greater detail below.

Acts in connection with care or treatment

Section 5 clarifies that in the event that 'P' is proven to lack capacity and the proposed act is in 'P's' best interests, any action which a professional may take requiring a 'hands-on' approach to care or treatment can be carried out without incurring any liability. This means that the professional carrying out the care is placed in the same position that they would have been in if 'P' had had capacity and had consented to the treatment. Section 6 permits restraint as long as the person carrying out the restraint 'reasonably believes it is necessary to do the act in order to prevent harm to P' (6(2)) and the restraint is a proportionate response to the likelihood and severity of that harm (s3 (a) and (b)).

Payment and expenditure

The Act makes provision for situations whereby if goods or services are provided to 'P', if 'P' lacks capacity he must still pay 'a reasonable price for them' (s7). Anyone who incurs a cost whilst carrying out a task in connection with care or treatment is also entitled to 'pledge P's credit' for that purpose (s8(1)(a)) or to claim that cost back from 'P' (s8(2)).

CASE STUDY 6.1, PART 2

Mrs Jones' family have become increasingly concerned at their mother's frequent inability to remember appointments and people's names. They persuade her to see her GP who sends her for tests. A diagnosis of vascular dementia is confirmed. What would be a sensible thing to do at this stage?

Lasting Powers of Attorney

One of the most significant provisions of the MCA, Lasting Powers of Attorney (LPA), allows one to appoint another person to make decisions on one's behalf if one should lose the capacity to make those decisions oneself (sections 9–14).

There are two different types of LPA which can be made: LPA for personal welfare and/or LPA for property and affairs. Both have to be made whilst the maker has capacity and they cannot be made until the maker reaches the age of 18. The maker can make either or both and can appoint more than one Attorney. If there is more than one then the maker will have specified whether the Attorneys can make decisions separately or whether they have to make them jointly.

Depending on the range of powers which the maker has donated to the Attorney, the Personal Welfare Attorney may be able to consent to various medical treatments and make decisions about residence.

The Property and Affairs Attorney may be able to make decisions regarding bank accounts, property and investments. It is possible for the Property and Affairs Attorney to act alongside the maker in certain circumstances before they have lost capacity.

Both types of Attorney are limited in the powers they exercise. They are bound by all of the provisions of the Act including the statutory principles and any decision they make on behalf of 'P' has to be in 'P's' best interests.

The Lasting Power of Attorney has to be registered at the Office of the Public Guardian (OPG) before it becomes a legally binding and actionable document. There is a fee for this. However, LPAs can be made online via the OPG website which has a specific tool for this purpose. There are certain requirements to complete before it can be registered such as having the document witnessed. More information is available via the OPG.

Anyone who is approached by an individual claiming to hold Power of Attorney on another's behalf should not take that information at face value. The original document or a certified copy should be seen. The document should be stamped at the bottom of the page by the OPG. If it is not stamped then it is not registered and thus not binding. Any decision at this stage would need to follow the best interests process. If it is not possible to see the document then a search of the OPG register can be requested.

CASE STUDY **6.1,** *PART* **3**

It comes to light that Mrs Jones was approached by a builder who told her that he could see her roof was in need of urgent repairs. He persuaded her to commission him to undertake the repairs and took her to an ATM in order to remove money. She doesn't feel able to refuse him.

What parts of the Act might be relevant here?

The Court of Protection and Court Appointed Deputies

The Court of Protection is a division of the High Court and has the power to make declarations about and decisions for 'P'. Declarations might include whether 'P' has capacity or not or the lawfulness of an action done to 'P'.

Decisions might include where 'P' is to live, who 'P' might have contact with or whether 'P' should continue to receive certain types of treatment. The Court may make decisions about these matters as a 'one-off' incident or alternatively it might appoint someone called a Court Appointed Deputy to make these decisions. As with Attorneys above, Deputies are subject to the provisions of the Act and have to make decisions in 'P's' best interests.

The Court also has the power to revoke Attorneys where, to the Court's satisfaction, it is proven that the Attorney is not acting in 'P's' best interests or where there is evidence that the LPA was made under duress or otherwise fraudulently.

The actions of the Court are covered in sections 16 to 23 of the Act.

Advance Decisions to Refuse Treatment

No-one has the right to demand specific treatment or types of treatment. However, sections 24 to 26 cover an individual's ability to specify, in advance of losing capacity, what specific treatments they might wish not to have once they lose capacity and cannot consent or refuse for themselves.

An Advance Decision to Refuse Treatment (ADRT) can deal with fairly minor treatments such as pain relief, across the spectrum to major treatments including the right to refuse life-sustaining treatments. ADRTs have to be 'valid' and 'applicable' but can be made verbally for most treatments although it is suggested that it is a good idea to write them down. However, an ADRT for life-sustaining treatment has to be in writing, signed by 'P', witnessed by a third party and contain a statement to the effect that the decision stands even if 'P's' life is at risk.

CASE STUDY *6.1*, PART *4*

Unfortunately Mrs Jones loses capacity to make her own decisions before it is possible to create a Lasting Power of Attorney or an ADRT. It becomes increasingly obvious that Mrs Jones is no longer able to live on her own in her own home. A decision needs to be made about where she should live. Who will make that decision and how?

Independent Mental Capacity Advocates

One of the safeguards contained in the Act is that for certain decisions, if 'P' is 'unbefriended', then the decision cannot be made unless an Independent Mental Capacity Advocate or IMCA has been appointed for 'P'.

The Code of Practice in Chapter 10 states, 'The purpose of the IMCA service is to help particularly vulnerable people who lack the capacity to make important decisions about serious medical treatment and changes of accommodation and who have no family of friends that it would be appropriate to consult about those decisions' (p178). The chapter emphasises throughout that it is the appropriateness of the consultee which is important, not the fact that one exists.

Lacking an appropriate person to consult, decisions cannot be made about serious medical treatment or about a long-term move in accommodation unless an IMCA has been commissioned.

The role of the IMCA primarily is to try and find out what 'P's' wishes and feelings about the decision in question would have been and provide that information to the decision-maker. In order to do this they can interview 'P', any relevant others in 'P's' life who might have information, read care records, investigate alternative options if any and feed any relevant information into the decision-making process (sections 35–41).

Ill-treatment or neglect

Section 44 of the Act makes it an offence for someone providing care to 'P' to ill-treat or wilfully neglect 'P'. The maximum penalty on conviction on indictment is 5 years imprisonment or a fine or both.

Deprivation of Liberty Safeguards

A later addition to the MCA, becoming active in 2009, the Deprivation of Liberty Safeguards or DoLS apply in hospitals and care homes where people are being given care and treatment in circumstances which might amount to a breach of their rights under Articles 5(1) and 5(4) of the European Convention on Human Rights (ECHR). This follows on from a case whereby a man who lacked capacity to consent to admission to a psychiatric hospital was admitted without the use of the Mental Health Act 1983 under common law. The European Court of Human Rights judged that the lack of a procedure for the admission of compliant yet incapacitated persons was a breach of their rights (*HL v UK* [2004] 40 EHRR 761).

In *P (by his litigation friend the Official Solicitor) v Cheshire West and Chester Council and another: P & Q (by their litigation friend the Official Solicitor) v Surrey County Council* [2014] UKSC 19 the Supreme Court has clarified that anyone who is confined somewhere for a not negligible period of time who cannot consent to that confinement and where the confinement is the responsibility of the state and in circumstances where the person is under continuous supervision and control and is not free to leave is, in fact, deprived of their liberty. In order to protect the individual such a deprivation of liberty needs to be authorised. In hospitals and care homes in England (there being some differences in Wales) this will be done by a local authority under the DoLS process following an assessment by a Best Interests Assessor (BIA) and a doctor. Outside of hospitals and care homes, including 'P's' home, an application to the Court of Protection may be required.

DoLS are supported by the Mental Capacity Act 2005: Deprivation of Liberty Safeguards Code of Practice to supplement the main Mental Capacity Act 2005 Code of Practice.

Part 2: Assessment of capacity and best interests decisions

Assessment of capacity

The first principle, as shown above, states that 'A person must be assumed to have capacity unless it is established that he lacks capacity' (1(2)). This so-called 'presumption of capacity' can cause problems for professionals working with vulnerable people who may come to that professional's attention because of an indication that decisions which they are making or actions which they are taking are somehow 'wrong' or 'problematic'. The identification of a decision as 'wrong' or 'problematic' may give rise to a belief that the person is not going to be able to make their own decisions generally and therefore to an assumption of a lack of capacity.

A good starting point can be a simple conversation between the individual and the professional. This is often enough to identify whether 'P' can make the decision or not and if it is felt unlikely that they can, indicates a requirement for a formal assessment.

It has to be remembered that capacity is time and decision specific. One cannot say that because 'P' has a diagnosis or a certain condition then 'P' lacks capacity to make decisions. If a decision has to be made the question should be asked, 'Can "P" make this decision at this time?'

Anyone can assess capacity and, indeed, if it is proposed to take action on behalf of 'P' it has to be proven, 'on the balance of probabilities', that 'P' lacks capacity to make his or her own decision before action can be taken. Therefore the person proposing to take the action needs to carry out that assessment themselves. It is possible and often desirable to seek 'expert' input perhaps from a specialist such as a psychiatrist or psychologist but the actual decision as to capacity cannot be delegated to that 'expert'. Obviously there are situations where a more robust assessment may be carried out by someone who knows 'P' well rather than someone who is being asked to assess on a 'one-off' basis.

CASE STUDY 6.1, PART 5

The decision has been made that Mrs Jones should live in a residential care home in the long term. This is in her best interests. In the care home she will be protected from risks such as losing her way or wandering into traffic. She will be given appropriate food and fluid and personal care.

Jane Smith is her named worker. Mrs Jones needs help to get up in the morning and to wash and dress herself. Accordingly the care staff wash her face and decide what clothing she should wear. What provisions of the Act might be in play here?

The Act and the Code of Practice set out how such an assessment should be carried out. A two stage process is suggested. Stage 1, which is sometimes referred to as the 'diagnostic test or stage', asks, 'Does the person have an impairment of, or disturbance in, the functioning of their mind or brain?' (2008, p44). Examples of this may include stroke, dementia, significant learning disabilities, infections etc. If there is no impairment or disturbance then 'P' has capacity. The impairment may be permanent or temporary. A key thing to note here is that a formal diagnosis is not required.

Stage 2, sometimes known as the 'functional stage', asks a further question: 'Does the impairment or disturbance mean that the person is unable to make a specific decision when they need to?' (2008, p45). The assessor then checks whether 'P' can make the decision by clarifying whether he or she can (a) understand information about the decision to be made; (b) retain that information long enough to make the decision; (c) use or weight that information as part of the decision-making process; and (d) communicate the decision by whatever means necessary. Failure on any one of these points will indicate a lack of capacity.

Case law clarifies the wording of the Act and Code. In *PC & NC v City of York Council* [2013] EWCA Civ 478 the judges indicated that they thought the two stages should be carried out in reverse order and that the person's ability to make the decision should be clarified first. If it is then decided that they cannot make the decision, then the assessor needs to be sure that this is because of the impairment or disturbance in the functioning of the mind or brain and nothing else. This is known as the 'causative nexus' and actually follows the wording of the Act itself at section 2(1) rather than the Code of Practice.

Ruck-Keen *et al.* (2016a) state that as a result of this case and *Kings College NHS Foundation Trust v C and V* [2015] EWCOP 80 '... there are actually three elements to the test for capacity: (1) is the person unable to make a decision? If so; (2) is there an impairment or disturbance in the functioning of the person's mind or brain? If so; (3) is the person's inability to make the decision because of the identified impairment or disturbance?' (p6).

Understanding the relevant information does not require that 'P' understands everything there is to know. The key thing is to give 'P' 'relevant information'. Care needs to be taken that the information given is not too abstract. A common example cited here by Ruck-Keen *et al.* (2016a) suggests assessing 'P's' capacity to decide between living at home and in a care home '... by reference to what continuing to live at home would be like (for instance, what care package would the relevant local authority provide) and what living in a care home would be like' (p8). The Code of Practice (p46) suggests that relevant information might include 'the nature of the decision, the reason why the decision is needed and the likely effects of deciding one way or another, or of making no decision at all'.

Retaining the information requires that 'P' can keep the relevant information in their mind for as long as is necessary to make the decision and no longer. It may be the case that the information is lost five minutes after communicating the decision but that does not indicate a lack of capacity.

Justice Hedley in *The PCT v P, AH and the Local Authority* [2009] EW Misc 10 (COP) stated that the ability to use or weigh the relevant information was the ability 'to actually engage in the decision-making process itself and to be able to see the various parts of the argument and to relate the one to the other' (para 35). Care needs to be taken in this part of the process not to confuse the inability to use or weigh the information with the making of an unwise decision (s1(4)). 'P' may not agree with the advice of professionals and indeed 'P' may be making a decision which the professionals could never see themselves making in similar circumstances but that does not mean that 'P' lacks capacity to make the decision.

It is again not necessary for 'P' to be able to use or weigh every piece of information. It is possible for 'P' to be able to use and weigh enough elements of the relevant information to make a capacitous decision. Where 'P' is able to use or weigh information, the weight which 'P' attaches to the information is for 'P' to decide. It is important to remember that 'P' will have his or her own set of morals or values which may not be the same as those of the assessor.

In communicating the decision, 'P' should be encouraged to use whatever mechanism he or she requires. Sometimes this may well be via speech but on other occasions it might require the writing down of the decision or the use of specialist tools or aids.

Fluctuating capacity

Fluctuating capacity can sometimes occur where cognitive impairments become more or less serious over time. This may be a matter of days or weeks such as in bi-polar disorder or over the course of a single day. Many older people with dementia are significantly less impaired in the morning for instance. The Act and Code of Practice require the assessment of capacity to be carried out at a time when it is likely that 'P' will be most able.

The first consideration in such cases is, 'Can the decision wait until "P" can make it themselves?' If it can then this is what should happen. This also applies in situations where 'P's' loss of capacity is likely to be temporary, for instance in the case of serious infections. In this instance it would be appropriate to make a decision about the treatment which may be required but to leave any other decision until 'P' can make it themselves.

If the decision cannot reasonably wait then it is important to take the minimum irreversible actions necessary in order to promote 'P's' recovery and protect their best interests. If a series of repeated decisions is required such as management of property and affairs or litigation, Ruck-Keen *et al.* '... suggest legal advice is sought wherever it appears that a person appears to have fluctuating capacity to take such decisions, because the consequences for the person may be very grave if they are assessed as having capacity in this regard when, in reality, this is only true for a very short period of time' (2016a, p14).

Coercion

Case law demonstrates that the Court can use its inherent jurisdiction in cases where adults at risk may come before it.

> *'Inherent jurisdiction' is a term used to describe the power of the High Court to hear any case which comes before it unless legislation or a rule has limited that power or granted jurisdiction to some other court or tribunal to hear the case. This means that the High Court has the power to hear a broad range of cases including those in relation to the welfare of adults, so long as the case is not already governed by procedures set out in rules or legislation.*

(Social Care Institute for Excellence, 2014)

Inherent jurisdiction is not normally used for people lacking capacity as they would fall under the auspices of the MCA. However, if there is a dispute about the person's capacity or if the person has capacity but cannot make a decision freely because of coercion or undue influence then the Court can be asked to intervene using its inherent jurisdiction.

An example of such a case is *A Local Authority v DL* [2010] EWHC 2675 (Fam): [2011] EWHC 1022 (Fam): [2012] EWCA Civ 253. In this case it was alleged that a man was mistreating his elderly parents who, at the outset, were judged to have capacity to make decisions. The local authority sought an order from the High Court to prevent that mistreatment including assaulting or threatening to assault his parents and preventing him trying to persuade his parents to sign over their home to him. Inherent jurisdiction may be useful in cases where scam victims are assessed as having capacity to decide to participate in the scam, yet there is evidence of coercion or undue influence affecting their decision-making or compromising their capacity.

Making 'best interests' decisions

It is necessary to remember that finding of a lack of capacity does not automatically mean that a decision has to be made via the best interests 'process'. The first requirement, if a decision has to be made, is to identify whether there is anyone else who could make it. In this context, this means an Attorney appointed under the provisions of a Lasting Power of Attorney or a Deputy appointed by the Court, both of which are described above. Whilst they are charged with acting in 'P's' best interests an Attorney or Deputy might have the required powers.

An alternative to this, if it is a treatment decision, is to seek the existence of a valid and applicable ADRT in which 'P' may have stated his or her wishes in relation to refusal of treatment. It is only after these steps have been exhausted that a best interests decision should be made.

The Act in s4 sets out some requirements that must be considered in determining best interests and the Code of Practice develops this further into a checklist which decision-makers should follow. However, before commencing this process it is important to remember that the principles of the Act continue to apply, especially the requirement to take all practicable steps to help the person make their own decision and to keep 'P' at the centre of the process.

Baroness Hale and colleagues in *Aintree University NHS Hospitals Trust v James* [2014] UKSC 67 emphasised that 'the purpose of the best interests test is to consider matters from the patient's point of view' (para 45). The final decision which is reached should be the decision which is right for the person themselves, not the decision which the assessor believes is the right one.

The best interests checklist can be found in Chapter 5 of the Code of Practice but can be summarised as follows:

The person undertaking the process:

- Must not make assumptions about the person's best interests on the basis of their age, appearance, condition or an aspect of their behaviour.

- Must try to identify all the circumstances relating to the decision which would be relevant to the person themselves.

- Must consider whether the person is likely to regain capacity. If so, and a decision can wait, it should.

- Must do whatever is reasonably practicable to help and encourage the person to participate in the process and in any act done for them.

- Must try to find out the person's views including their past and present wishes and feelings; any beliefs or values that would be likely to influence the decision; and any other factors the person would be likely to consider if they were able to.

- Must consult other people if it is practicable and appropriate to do so. People to consult might include but are not limited to: anyone previously named by the person as being someone to consult; anyone engaged in caring for the person or close relatives, friends or others who take an interest in the person's welfare; any Attorney or Court Appointed Deputy.

- Must consult an IMCA if the decision is about serious medical treatment or where the person should live and there is no one appropriate to consult with.

- Must not be motivated in any way by a desire to bring about the person's death if the decision relates to life-sustaining treatment.

- Must avoid restricting the person's rights.

- Must take all the information into account and weigh it up.

It is important to remember that in the consultation process, 'P's right to confidentiality must still be adhered to'.

In undertaking this process, it is useful to set out the options that might be available in some form of table highlighting the positives and negatives of each. This might include the risks and benefits of each option as well as the likelihood and seriousness of those risks and benefits occurring. Any conclusions drawn need to clearly identify where one element outweighed another or where particular weight was placed upon an individual aspect. Any dispute about best interests or the decision reached may ultimately need to be referred to the Court of Protection if no resolution can be reached.

Not all best interest decisions are going to be made in daylight with ready availability of consultees. The principle behind best interests is a reasonable belief that an act or decision is in 'P's' best interests. As Ruck-Keen *et al.* remind us, 'What will be required [in order] to have a reasonable belief as to a person's best interests in the context of an A&E department at 3:00 am will be very different to what may be required in the context of a decision whether an elderly person with dementia should move from their home of 60 years into a care home' (2016b, p3).

Key learning points

- Mental capacity is the ability to make a decision (MCA Code of Practice 2007, p41).

- The first principle of the MCA is that everyone can make their own decisions unless it is proven otherwise. This is known as the 'presumption of capacity' and is set out in section 1, subsection 2 of the Act.

- A difficult concept to work with linked to risk taking is that people have the right to make 'unwise decisions' without calling their decision-making abilities into question. This can be a tricky area in terms of protecting individuals from involvement in financial scams.

- A significant provision of the MCA is that of Lasting Powers of Attorney (LPA), which allows one to appoint another person to make decisions on one's behalf if they should lose the capacity to make decisions themselves.

- Fluctuating capacity can sometimes occur where cognitive impairments become more or less serious over time. The Act and Code of Practice require the assessment of capacity to be carried out at a time when it is likely that 'P' will be most able.

- If there is a dispute about the person's capacity or if the person has capacity but cannot make a decision freely because of coercion or undue influence, then the Court can be asked to intervene using its inherent jurisdiction.

- In some circumstances it may be necessary to apply to the Court of Protection to make the decision in the person's best interests in terms of their financial protection.

FURTHER READING

Ashton, G. and Bielanska, C. (2014) *Elderly People and the Law*, 2nd edn. Bristol: Jordans.

Barber, P., Brown, R. and Martin, D. (2015) *The Mental Capacity Act 2005: A Guide for Practice*, 3rd edn. London: Sage/ Learning Matters.

Graham, M. and Cowley, J. (2015) *A Practical Guide to Mental Capacity Act 2005: Putting the Principles of the Act into Practice*. London: Jessica Kingsley.

House of Lords Select Committee on the Mental Capacity Act 2005 (2014) *Mental Capacity Act 2005: Post-Legislative Scrutiny. Report of Session 2013–14*. London: TSO. www.publications.parliament.uk/pa/ld201314/ldselect/ ldmentalcap/139/139.pdf

Ministry of Justice (2008) *Mental Capacity Act 2005: Deprivation of Liberty Safeguards Code of Practice to Supplement the Main Mental Capacity Act 2005 Code of Practice*. London: TSO.

Ruck-Keene, A. (ed) (2015) *Assessment of Mental Capacity*, 4th edn. The British Medical Association and The Law Society. London: The Law Society.

Ruck-Keene, A., Edwards, K., Eldergill, A. and Miles, S. (2014) *The Court of Protection Handbook: A User's Guide*. London: Legal Action Group.

Chapter 7

Developing an understanding of the National Trading Standards Scams Team

Louise Baxter, National Trading Standards Scams Team Manager, with contributions from Jodie Gordon and Rebekah Salmon

---

CHAPTER OUTCOMES

As a result of completing this chapter you will:

- Understand the history of National Trading Standards (NTS) and the National Trading Standards Scams Team (NTS Scams Team).

- Understand the role of local trading standards and the NTS Scams Team in addressing financial abuse by scams.

- Understand ways of supporting the victims of scams.

- Understand the legislation which can be used to combat scams.

The development of National Trading Standards (NTS) and the National Trading Standards Scams Team (NTS Scams Team)

National Trading Standards was set up by the government in 2012 as part of changes to the national consumer protection landscape. NTS provide leadership, influence, support and resources to help combat consumer and business detriment nationally, regionally and locally, bringing together trading standards representatives from England and Wales to prioritise, fund and coordinate national and regional enforcement cases (National Trading Standards, 2016). Funding to support the NTS is provided by the Department for Business, Energy and Industrial Strategy (BEIS) and the Food Standards Agency (FSA). National Trading Standards recognise the importance of co-ordination activities, prioritising case selection and deployment of resources. They ensure that enforcement action is co-ordinated to achieve the greatest level of protection for consumers and businesses, and gather intelligence from around the country to protect businesses and consumers from criminal activity. Key priorities are tackling e-crime, mass marketing scams, doorstep crime, illegal money lending and other enforcement issues that go beyond local authority boundaries.

NTS Teams include those shown in Figure 7.1.

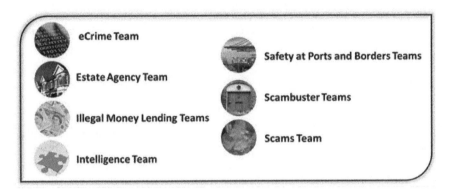

Figure 7.1 Composition of National Trading Standards Teams.

Local trading standards

Local authority trading standards professionals act on behalf of local consumers and businesses, advising on and enforcing laws that govern the way consumers and businesses buy, sell, rent and hire goods and services. There are around 200 trading standards services within the UK, each prioritising work according to the steer of their local authority. However, the focus of local trading standards is safeguarding the interests of consumers and businesses in their local areas.

The legislative areas covered include those shown in Figure 7.2.

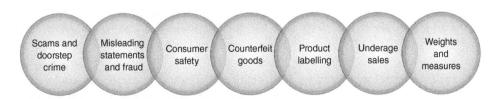

Figure 7.2 Trading standards legislative areas.

Trading standards remit

- Enforce legislation relating to the supply of goods and services.

- Take action against traders who break the law.

- Advise and educate traders who may not be aware that they are breaking the law.

- Offer advice and help to consumers.

- Take informal action on less serious cases in the form of giving advice, guidance and educating traders who have broken the law and making sure they do not do it again.

- Take formal action on the more serious cases in the form of prosecuting in criminal courts, issuing cautions, applying for injunctions, issuing statutory notices, entering premises and seizing goods and/or documents.

- Assist consumers to take the trader to court where there is substantial evidence.

- Carry out routine inspections.

- Check price displays in retail premises and ensure that they are accurate.

- Protect consumers and traders.

(UK Trading Standards, 2016)

The cuts to spending on public services following the financial crash of 2007/8 and subsequent austerity measures in the UK and elsewhere (discussed in Chapter 1) have had a profound impact on trading standards. The 2016 CTSI Workforce Survey highlights year on year cuts in resources for trading standards services across Great Britain. Austerity has continued to bite, leading to the loss of a further 12 per cent of trading standards staff since 2014, in addition to the 45 per cent drop identified over the previous 5 years. The total spend on local authority trading standards services has fallen to an estimated £124 million, down from £213 million in 2009. This means that trading standards now costs an average of £1.99 per person per year – less than the cost of some Sunday newspapers (CTSI, 2016).

The National Trading Standards Scams Team: our aims

Action to address the huge, and growing, impact of mass marketing scams is essential: each year scams cause between £5 and £10 billion of detriment to UK consumers. This figure comprises the estimated £5.8 billion lost to mass marketing fraud (Lonsdale *et al.*, 2016) and the further £4 billion lost to doorstep crime (see Chapter 8). The NTS Scams Team statistics of December 2016 reveal that the average victim of mass marketing fraud loses £2333. Multiplying this figure by the 3.25 million annual scam victims (University of Portsmouth, 2016) results in losses of £7.7 billion. These sums demonstrate the substantial impact of scams on economies and markets by undermining consumer trust in legitimate businesses. The word 'scam' potentially hides the true seriousness of the fraud and crime suffered by victims as discussed in Chapter 3.

Scams make victims part with their money and personal details by intimidating them or promising cash, prizes, services and fictitious high returns on investment.

(NTS Scams Team, 2016)

The National Trading Standards Scams Team (NTS Scams Team) was formed in 2012 as part of the national response to scams. Stakeholders, including Royal Mail and the Metropolitan Police, worked with trading standards to identify victims of mass marketing fraud (MMF). A 'suckers list' (a list of current or potential scam targets traded between scammers as discussed in Chapter 3) had been seized with over 100,000 names on it. These victims were likely to be 'silent' (only 5 per cent of victims report the fact they have responded to a scam (OFT, 2006)) and probably unaware they had been defrauded. Research identified a huge gap in the system of identification and support for victims, through which they were falling, and the National Scams Hub was an innovative idea born out of frustration and the desire to improve the fractured process of identifying and supporting the 'silent' victims of MMF.

In 2014 the National Scams Hub became the National Trading Standards Scams Team and is now a national priority funded by the NTS and BEIS. The NTS Scams Team has significantly improved the fractured process of identifying and supporting scam victims by coordinating work across England and Wales with trading standards and partner agencies.

Scams vary in type, nature and targeted victim population (as discussed in Chapter 3). There are different organisations which focus on these different types of scams, victims and impacts which results in a fractured response at national and local levels. This has obscured the recognition by society of the seriousness of scamming, which is fraudulent, criminal, financially abusive behaviour often targeted specifically at disadvantaged consumers or those in periods of vulnerability.

The aims of the National Trading Standards Scams Team are:

- To **IDENTIFY** victims of scams.
- To **INTERVENE** and protect victims from further victimisation.
- To **INVESTIGATE** criminal activity.
- To **INFORM** local authorities and agencies on how to work with and support scam victims.
- To **INFLUENCE** people at local, regional and national levels to **TAKE A STAND AGAINST SCAMS**.

The team receives information from a range of sources, their own investigations and over 40 partner agencies that **IDENTIFY** potential scam victims. This includes 'suckers/victims lists' and direct partner referrals from organisations that come into contact with potential scam victims such as financial institutions, mail providers, charities and other key partners. The NTS Scams Team then contacts the local trading standards service of those silent victims and enters into partnership agreements with them, which include a variety of ways in which local authorities can work together to **INTERVENE** and support their identified victims. Information is gathered about victims and effective interventions

Figure 7.3 Examples of NTS Scams Team campaigns.

enabling the team to **INFORM** local authorities and partner agencies about the most effective ways to work with and support scam victims.

The NTS Scams Team acts on information received from various sources, including in-house projects such as Friends Against Scams, Mail Marshals and campaigns to **INVESTIGATE** the path of scam mail. Through tracing the path of money sent in response to scams, the team have had well documented success (Lonsdale *et al.*, 2016) and continue to act on new leads to tackle fraudulent activities. The team works with partners, financial institutions to trace the money, liaising internationally to identify and stop it at source. The team also works with mail providers to stop the mail from entering the postal system and reaching the victims.

When the team started in 2012, only 6 per cent of local authorities were undertaking work to identify and support local scam victims. By the end of 2016 the team had signed up 181 local authorities, 91 per cent of the UK, gathering victim information and committing to proactively use this data to support people. Part of the agreement is that local authorities feed back their findings to the NTS Scams Team, including the individual's age, the detriment experienced, the savings made by the individual following trading standards intervention and the result of intervention. This data enables the team to observe patterns, develop strategies and share best practice.

The NTS Scams Team aims to raise awareness of scams by producing resources and leading campaigns to **INFLUENCE** people at local, regional and national levels. This includes a wide range of active projects and campaigns covering a variety of needs and producing excellent results. This includes the Friends against Scams initiative which aims to prevent and protect people from becoming victims of scams by empowering communities to 'Take a Stand Against Scams.'

CASE STUDY **7.1**

Action in practice

Taking a stand against scams: Friends Against Scams

Jodie Gordon, Project Assistant, National Trading Standards Scams Team

Through the work of the NTS Scams Team, it became apparent that there was a need for a scams campaign which went beyond simply raising awareness. The team recognised that

(Continued)

CASE STUDY *7.1* (CONT.)

many awareness-raising campaigns existed and had achieved varying success, but most related to more complex scams such as cyber scams and advised consumers how they could protect themselves from these types of scams in the future. The scale of financial scams is believed to be under reported and therefore misunderstood by the wider public, which in some cases results in the issue being trivialised. In order to combat this, the NTS Scams Team began to plan a campaign with a difference: Friends Against Scams.

Friends Against Scams is different because it aims to produce outcomes which will reach beyond consumers simply protecting themselves, encouraging them to also look out for others within their family and community. There are many tiers to Friends Against Scams, first and foremost are 'Friends' – anyone can become a Friend by attending a face to face awareness session or by completing the online learning. Both approaches support learning about a range of scams including postal, telephone, online and doorstep crime. In addition to this, the sessions highlight the possible signs of those who may have fallen victim to a scam and how to report or deal with them. This element of Friends Against Scams is vital as it is the tool which enables people to then proactively look out for others as well as themselves, giving everybody the potential to make a difference.

To highlight the scale of the problem, the Friends' training also includes real case studies of scam victims, demonstrating the devastating effects caused by scams. The final part of the Friends Against Scams session asks participants to make a pledge to Take a Stand Against Scams.

Alongside 'Friends', there are SCAMchampions and SCAMbassadors within the initiative. A SCAMchampion is someone who has already become a Friend but feels that they would like to do a little more, attending a further session to look at the Friends Against Scams resources in detail, and exploring how they can set up their own Friends' sessions in their own communities. SCAMchampions are equipped with the knowledge and resources to spread the Friends Against Scams initiative far and wide. SCAMbassadors are MPs, senior officials or people who are able to use their influence to raise the profile of scams and help to deliver the Friends Against Scams message both locally and on a national level. The unique element of Friends Against Scams is how the initiative works in a multitude of settings – the public, local authorities, organisations – both local and national, and other groups.

To support the initiative further, Friends Against Scams has a dedicated website, and completion of the simple online learning is an alternative to attending face to face awareness sessions. The Friend Against Scams website adds to the potential for the initiative to have wide reach, supporting the aim of raising awareness and encouraging people to talk about scams and commit to taking action.

If every Friend plays their part Friends Against Scams can lead the way in tackling the issue of scams and preventing people falling victim in the future.

What will you do?

Once you have become a Friend Against Scams, what will you pledge to do? Some ideas include:

- *Tell five people about the Friends Against Scams initiative.*
- *Educate and talk to people about scams.*
- *Share your Friends Against Scams status on social media.*
- *Look out for people who are at risk of being a scam victim in your community.*
- *Campaign for change – write to your local MP asking them promote scams awareness.*
- *Actively support your local fight against scams by setting up or taking part in a scam awareness activity or event in your local area.*
- *Challenge attitudes about scam victims and help to stamp out the stigma of this commonly misunderstood problem by talking about scams and influencing people to consider scams from a different point of view.*

One attendee at a recent Friends Against Scams awareness session reported: 'I was so inspired by today's session that I am going to hold a coffee morning at home to tell my friends and neighbours about Friends Against Scams and the scale of the problem.'

Remember, everyone can make a difference in their own way.

ACTIVITY 7.1

Complete the Friends Against Scams online learning at **www.friendagainst scams.org.uk**

What does the NTS Scams Team do: practical solutions and victim support

Feedback from scam victims reveals that at the end of the 2015/16 financial year consumer detriment and savings were as shown in Figure 7.4.

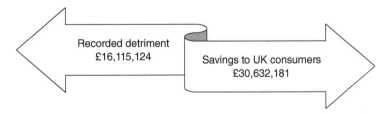

Recorded detriment
£16,115,124

Savings to UK consumers
£30,632,181

Figure 7.4 Consumer detriment and savings, 2015/16.

Financial losses do not fully reflect all of the costs that scam victims often bear. For some victims, the risks extend beyond loss of personal savings or funds to include physical risks, loss of their homes, depression and increased suicide risk.

The NTS Scams Team's evidence shows that the average age of a scams victim is 75, and victims may repeatedly respond to scams over a number of years, losing huge amounts of money. Donaldson (2003) found evidence that people who are defrauded in their own homes are 2.5 times more likely to either die or go into residential care within a year of the event, in comparison to non-victims.

The problem of scamming is growing: there are *300,000 potential victims on the NTS Scams Team database with an expectation that this will exceed 1 million in the fore-seeable future.*

This means more has to be done.

DISCUSSION POINT 7.1

Consider ways in which this number of victims can be supported.

(It should also be noted that the Office for National Statistics fraud statistics for England and Wales do not include trading standards statistics. However, the NTS Scams Team is currently working on this issue at a national level.)

CASE STUDY 7.2

Multi-agency approach

Community Wardens work in partnership with Kent County Council Trading Standards, police and local authorities and have campaigned to prevent and reduce scam crime.

Whilst working on the 'Stop the Criminals responsible for scams' project, the Community Wardens visited more than 600 scam victims who had been identified on the NTS 'suckers list'. During these visits, the wardens completed a questionnaire with each resident giving feedback to monitor the progress of the 'Stop the Criminals responsible for scams' project and provide the National Trading Standards Scams Team with the feedback needed to tackle national scams issues.

The Community Wardens also deliver scams awareness training to banks and post offices, ensuring an effective and successful referral process is in place.

Support to local authorities

The NTS National Scams Team gathers evidence and practical solutions about appropriate and successful interventions from local authorities. The team then shares this information with local trading standards departments across the country so they have access to models of best practice, information, strategies and advice which, in light of diminishing funding to local trading standards, makes them better able and more likely to support victims.

The NTS Scams Team provides support to local authorities in the form of:

- E-learning
- Toolkits
- Online forum
- Fortnightly scam alert
- Monthly newsletter
- National campaign material.

They support local pilots, providing best practice examples on how to take a multi-agency approach, specifically supporting Against Scams Partnerships to encourage a multi-agency approach to scams. The team co-ordinates the Mail Marshals scheme.

The Mail Marshal scheme

A Mail Marshal is any resident in the UK who receives scam mail, and wants to put it to good use. Mail Marshals are responsible for collecting scam mail so that it can be utilised as evidence in future investigative and enforcement work for the NTS Scams Team. Mail Marshals may even be asked to be witnesses (if they would like to assist further), but this is not mandatory.

Becoming a Mail Marshal can be rewarding and fulfilling work. Feedback demonstrates that in many cases it has helped Mail Marshals to:

- Save money
- Take control of their situation
- Improve self-confidence
- Reduce clutter in the home
- Assist with investigations
- Reduce the temptation to respond
- Increases awareness of scams
- Educate and help others
- See a reduction in the scam mail they receive.

This scheme is an example of empowerment in action. Each month Mail Marshals receive a newsletter and someone is declared Mail Marshal of the Month.

Mail Marshal of the Month

How long have you been receiving scam letters? Why do you think it started?

I don't know why it started. I just started receiving them about a year and a half ago.

What type of scams are they, i.e. clairvoyant, prize draw, catalogue, romance?

I get them all! People who see visions of me on their wall. I get catalogues and prize draws I never entered.

How long have you been a Mail Marshal and what do you like about it?

I've been a Mail Marshal for a month now and my level of post has dropped considerably. I used to get 10–12 letters a day. I like feeling like I can help others and help make them aware of this problem. I was heartbroken for the Think Jessica woman – she just didn't catch on that people can be like that.

Do you ever feel tempted to respond to scam criminals? Why or why not?

I did in the beginning. I didn't realise it was a scam right away and responded to the first letter, which felt like a great big hug. Then I suddenly got others, all from the Netherlands, wanting £40 and I put the pieces together. Something was not right.

What advice can you give someone who is being taken for a scam?

Go speak to someone about it. Don't keep it to yourself. Don't let it happen to someone else. People need to be aware of the problem to avoid it. Even if it's just one letter – ask for help.

Letter from a Mail Marshal's relative

Dear NTS Scams Team,

My father and I have been completing Mail Marshal forms for some time. Since I moved in with him and we did this together he has responded to very few. At its peak he received an average of 25 a day and this has reduced to 1–4 a day. Installing BT call guardian has also helped by blocking calls from these companies.

I'm pleased to hear that other countries are helping to track down these criminals.

My Dad died on 5/11/16 and he never completely believed that every one of these letters were a scam, despite all the evidence to the contrary. He responded for over 10 years and must have spent thousands of pounds.

That I'm afraid is the problem.

The help given by trading standards and yourselves has been invaluable. There will however be other people whose families will not know the extent of the issue. I feel that until Royal Mail has permission from the government to stop delivering this mail, this fraud will continue.

It was very difficult as a family watching my lovely Dad being exploited by these people.

Thank you for your support which helped to bring this issue under control.

Call blocker work – Rebekah Salmon, National Trading Standards Scams Team

In 2015 the government announced a £3.5 million package to help stop nuisance calls (Hancock, 2016). This included a government commitment of £500,000 to provide free call blocking technology to people at the highest risk of financial harm and personal distress from nuisance calls. The NTS Scams Team was identified as the body to carry out the work and procured user end call blocking devices for distribution to vulnerable people nationwide. They piloted a Call Blocker Project in January 2015, during which 100 Call Blockers were distributed to over 40 local authorities who installed the devices in consumers' homes. The pilot concluded in April 2016, and over 30,000 scam and nuisance calls had been blocked. One consumer received 23 nuisance/scam calls in a single day. Approximately 93 per cent of consumers felt safer in their own homes as a result of using the Call Blocker.

The types of calls received included market research and surveys, accident claims, robot calls, silent calls, lottery scams, computer scams, PPI claims, Sky scams, TPS scams and insurance claims, etc. The largest volume of these unwanted calls originated in the UK, however, other countries included Canada, USA, France, Nigeria, Australia, the Netherlands, France, Bermuda, Tonga and Chile to name but a few.

The NTS Scams Team is using this pilot to drive forward this Department of Culture, Media and Sport call blocking project to ensure that UK consumers are protected in their homes from both scam and nuisance calls. Scam calls are those which have the intention of defrauding the receiver whilst also obtaining personal or financial details. Nuisance calls can be inconvenient, annoying, and occur where consent has not been given to receive such a call (this definition of nuisance calls has been devised by the NTS Scams Team). These include silent, robotic and persistent calls from call centres. For most people these calls cause distress and anxiety, but significantly more so for people who are made vulnerable by their circumstances, such as people who are socially isolated.

Unwanted telephone calls in the UK have increased over the last 5 years, becoming a nationally recognised issue. As a result the government has approved changes to legislation: in 2015, a legal threshold which previously required the Information Commissioner's Office (ICO) to prove that a call caused 'substantial damage or distress' in order for the offending company to be punished was removed (Vaizey, 2015). Alongside this, the ICO and Ofcom have been granted greater powers to disrupt and fine bad (i.e. aggressive sales calls or direct marketing calls to numbers registered with the Telephone Preference Service (TPS)) telephone practices made by companies.

The ICO has issued fines totalling almost £3.7 million to companies behind nuisance marketing. In 2016 the ICO fined firms responsible for more than 70 million calls and nearly 8 million spam texts (Vaizey, 2015). For example, in September 2015, Home Energy & Lifestyle Management Ltd (HELM) was fined £200,000 for making over 6 million nuisance calls as part of a massive automated call marketing campaign.

In 2015, the ICO received a total of 168,159 concerns about nuisance calls and texts, which was actually down by 4 per cent from 2014. This small fall from a record high in 2014 might be attributable to enforcement action by the ICO, Ofcom and the Claims Management Regulator and the widespread media coverage of nuisance calls in 2015. However, research shows just 2 per cent of people who received unwanted calls reported them, making it difficult to draw conclusions about either the extent of calls received and causes for any apparent fall in number (Which? 2016a). Further complexity to identifying the true number of scam calls received by consumers arises from reports being made to the ICO, Citizens Advice and Action Fraud.

Despite the work tackling scam and nuisance calls, vulnerable consumers, including some older people, are being purposefully targeted by unscrupulous companies. According to research vulnerable customers who have been utilising a Call Blocker device are receiving an average of 38 unwanted calls a month – that's 46 per cent higher than the 26 calls a month received by users of the standard box (Which? 2016a). One in five vulnerable people received more than 60 scam or nuisance calls a month; these calls are a scourge for many UK consumers.

Investigation work

The NTS Scams Team has devised successful enforcement strategies to deal with perpetrators of mass marketing scams who use UK based enablers. The team works closely with other enforcement bodies, mail providers and financial institutions and international enforcement bodies to tackle scam mail at source and prevent it reaching victims. Enablers range from accommodation address providers to consolidation houses and mail forwarding delivery offices.

The NTS Scams Team has detained several thousand pieces of mail, processing it and then returning money to the victims. This is often small amounts, but returning money to a consumer often allows trading standards officers to engage with victims and start building a relationship with them.

Enforcement and consumer protection legislation

The Consumer Protection from Unfair Trading Regulations (CPR) 2008

The regulations aim to protect consumers from unfair, misleading or aggressive selling practices. However, it could also be argued that this type of contact is simply a 'sharp practice' which builds on mainstream marketing techniques. The CPRs provide the framework to distinguish between the two. They are enforceable by trading standards.

There are three main sections in the Regulations:

- A general ban on unfair commercial practices (s3).

- A ban on misleading and aggressive practices which are assessed in light of the effect they have, or are likely to have, on the average consumer (s5–7).

- The list of commercial practices, which will always be unfair and are banned outright (CPR, schedule 1).

What is unfair?

Under the Regulations, a commercial practice is 'unfair' if it fits both of the following criteria:

- It falls below the good-faith standards of skill and care that a trader in that industry would be expected to exercise towards consumers.

- It affects, or is likely to affect, consumers' ability to make an informed decision about whether to purchase a particular product (s3).

A trader will be committing an offence under the Regulations if they knowingly or recklessly engage in an 'unfair' practice.

Misleading actions

To make scams attractive they often include misleading claims. It is an offence under Regulation 6 for traders to use misleading tactics to get consumers to spend money, or make some other transactional decision that they would not otherwise have made. Misleading actions include advertising goods that do not exist, or offering just a few items at the advertised price with no hope, or intention, of meeting large demand.

Traders are also banned from:

- Making misleading comparisons, for example: 'product A lasts twice as long as product B' if in fact Product A lasts only slightly longer.

- Giving false information about the characteristics of goods: for example, 'We only sell genuine, branded parts', when in reality they are selling non-branded spare parts, or whether a product needs servicing or replacing.

- Misleading consumers about their legal rights.

- Giving false or deceptive information about their business, status or qualifications.

If a trader has signed up to a code of practice (for example a garage might sign up to the Motor Industry Code of Practice for Service and Repair), but fails to follow the code, they could be in breach of the Regulations.

Misleading omissions

The Regulations offer protection against traders who are economical with the truth, or miss out key information that consumers need to make an informed decision. Traders must make sure the information is adequate, understandable, accessible and provided in a timely manner. This means information must be displayed clearly as obscure presentation is tantamount to an omission.

Sales tactics

Sales tactics can influence a consumer's decision. Traders who fail to take no for an answer, refuse to leave until a contract is signed, or use threatening behaviour will be committing an offence under Regulation 7 and possibly 3, 5 and 6. A commercial practice is considered aggressive if, by means of harassment, coercion or undue influence, it significantly impairs (or is likely to significantly impair) the average consumer's freedom of choice or conduct, which then leads the consumer to take a transactional decision that they would otherwise not have made. The legislation contains a list of criteria to help determine whether a commercial practice uses harassment, coercion, including physical force, or undue influence (Regulation 7).

The list of banned practices

In addition to tackling misleading and aggressive behaviour, the Regulations blacklist 31 specific practices, such as claiming something is free when it is not and persistent cold-calling (schedule 1 of the CPRs).

In the case of these blacklisted practices it is enough simply to demonstrate wrongdoing; there is no need to show that it influenced the consumer's decision in any way. A trader taking part in any of the blacklisted practices is committing a criminal offence.

The list of banned practices includes the following, each of which relate to techniques used by scammers:

- **Bait advertising** – luring the consumer with attractive advertising around special prices when the trader knows that he cannot offer that product, or only has a few in stock at that price.

- **Bait and switch** – promoting one product with the intention of selling you something else.

- **Limited offers** – falsely stating that a product will only be available for a very limited time, or that it will only be available on particular terms for a very limited time, in order to elicit an immediate decision and deprive consumers of sufficient opportunity or time to make an informed choice.

- **False free offers** – describing a product as free or without charge if the consumer has to pay anything other than the unavoidable cost of responding to the offer and collecting or paying for delivery of the item.

- **Pressure selling** – creating the impression that the consumer cannot leave the premises until a contract is formed.

- **Aggressive doorstep selling** – conducting personal visits to the consumer's home ignoring the consumer's request to leave or not to return.

(Which? 2016b)

Fraud Act 2006

Scams are FRAUD (see Chapter 3) and perpetrators can be prosecuted under the Fraud Act 2006.

Section 2 of the Fraud Act states:

A person is in breach of this section if he:

(a) *dishonestly makes a false representation, and*

(b) *intends, by making the representation –*

    (i) *to make a gain for himself or another, or*

    (ii) *to cause loss to another or to expose another to a risk of loss.*

A representation is false if:

(a) *it is untrue or misleading, and*

(b) *the person making it knows that it is, or might be, untrue or misleading.*

DISCUSSION POINT 7.2

How would you engage with a scam victim? What tactics would you use?

Working with victims

Making the initial visit

The NTS Scams Team recommends face to face visits for the most effective interventions, particularly for the initial visit.

Tips on how to engage with a scam victim

- Be highly sensitive to the victim and employ tact and empathy.

- Take a conversational approach instead of asking structured questions.

- Seek to sensitively obtain more information regarding the scams (e.g. timescales of victimisation/any contact details of criminals etc.) by asking informal and open questions.

- Try and establish if they are the victim of any other scams, e.g. doorstep scams, befriending, etc.

- Spend time listening to the consumer; do not judge them.

- Present them with different options, but allow and encourage them to make their own choices.

- Refrain from getting frustrated, interrupting them or finishing their sentences.

- Use honest, simple and caring language which makes them feel as if they're being empathised with and taken seriously.

After the meeting

- Leave a contact card.

- Encourage the victim to contact you after the first meeting if they remember more details about the things you've talked about.

- Leave plastic bags/envelopes with the victim to collect future scam mail.

- Arrange a follow-up visit to provide further support and to collect scam mail.

- Destroy scam mail.

- Optional: Sort through scam mail to collect any information and share this with the NTS Scams Team.

- Optional: Discuss with victim if they would consider signing up to be a Mail Marshal, in which they will be responsible for collecting, recording and returning their scam mail to the NTS Scams Team.

Intervention and follow-up visits

Every victim's situation is different and appropriate support and intervention depends on the individual's circumstances and needs. Intervention from the local authority must be taken in accordance with the Mental Capacity Act 2005 (discussed in Chapter 6), person-centred care and human rights principles.

The following list offers some possible next steps.

Steps for the victim to take

- Demonstrate to a victim how to identify and dispose of scam mail without opening it and how to shred their personal and financial information.

- Coach them to understand the dangers of giving out their personal or financial information.

- Coach them to confidently handle unwanted telephone calls and how to hang up without sounding rude.

Steps for the local authority to take

- Consider the Care Act 2014. Section 42(3) of the Care Act requires local authorities to make enquires, or ask others to make enquiries, when they think an adult with care and support needs may be at risk of abuse or neglect in their area and to find out what, if any, action may be needed. Scams and fraud constitute financial abuse (s42(4)).

- Consider contacting family/friends/neighbours with the individual's consent.

- If the consumer does not wish you to contact their family/friends/neighbours then consider a safeguarding alert through adult social care.

- Work with the individual to create a network of friends and family who can help to sort and filter out any scam mailings with the individual, which can then be removed and disposed of.

- Request permission to remove any existing scam mail (victim consent required).

- Sign up to the Mail/Telephone Preference Service. Signing up to these services will reduce the volume of mail and telephone calls. However, its effect on preventing criminals from contacting the victim will be limited: **http://www.tpsonline.org.uk/tps/index.html http://www.mpsonline.org.uk/mpsr/**

- Consider Mail Redirection, a chargeable service through Royal Mail. Follow the link for more information and pricing details: **https://www.royalmail.com/personal/receiving-mail/redirection**

- Consider using Mail Collect, a free service offered by Royal Mail.

- Attempt to have the victim's details removed from any mailing lists.

- Ensure that any ongoing charitable donations are being sent to genuine charities. Check the Registered Charity number against the official Charity Commission's website: **https://www.gov.uk/government/organisations/charity-commission**

- Suggest, if appropriate, a Lasting Power of Attorney.

- Change bank details (victim consent required).

- Change telephone number (victim consent required) as this can be a very effective way to break the cycle of victimisation.

- Consider the installation of a call blocking device.

- Consider if the victim would be an appropriate Mail Marshal and discuss this role and its responsibilities with the victim. Becoming a Mail Marshal can be very rewarding and fulfilling; it can sometimes fill the void where the victim previously used the time to respond to scam mail.

CASE STUDY 7.3

The National Trading Standards Scams Team referred a potential victim to trading standards. The trading standards officer made a background check of the potential victim and he was not known by adult social care, health team or trading standards.

(Continued)

A visit was made to Mr. B's home. He is 69 years old and is an educated man, who previously worked as an engineer. The trading standards officer (TSO) found the house full of scam mail.

Mr. B said that he started to receive scam mail 5 to 10 years ago, when he responded to an advert in the newspaper. It became apparent that he spends his time scrutinising the mail he receives. He initially told the TSO that he only responds to those which you can return with no obligation to purchase/pay. He has a full range of scam mail, mainly prize draws, unclaimed funds, lotteries, but also clairvoyants.

The TSO estimated that there were at least 3000 letters stacked up in the downstairs of the house. On the fireplace were a set of letters, which he told the officer were those he had ready to send back, but he didn't have the money for the stamps.

The TSO estimated Mr. B has lost more than £20k. Mr. B is now in financial difficulty, struggling to buy food, with unpaid direct debits and bounced cheques. There were also a number of loan application forms in the house.

The TSO told him quite directly that he needed to stop responding and registered him with the Mail Preference Service. The TSO referred him to safeguarding and a social worker visited him.

A second visit was made by the TSO with a police officer and they found 50 per cent of the mail had been cleared. The police officer explained to Mr. B that he was effectively funding organised crime. Mr. B suggested that we need to tell other people and agreed to deliver posters and postcards in his community area. He also asked the TSO to contact the sorting office and request that they stop delivering the scam mail to him. The TSO sent Mr. B posters and postcards and he rang asking for more, as he had more shops and churches to take them to. Mr. B's character has completely changed and he is happy and feeling positive about helping others that are in a similar situation.

Working with partners

The NTS Scams Team focuses on how to combat criminal activity associated with mail based mass marketing fraud by working with a wide range of key partners and agencies in the UK and internationally, such as trading standards partners, Royal Mail and other mail providers, and law enforcement and the banking sector to tackle the problem.

A recent case

NTS Scams Team worked internationally to investigate a Vancouver-based firm accused of transnational crime.

It is alleged that the company in question has been laundering cash raised through 'mail fraud schemes' for 20 years.

A Canadian payment processor became one of the many targets of an unprecedented crackdown on global mail fraud. The frauds raked in millions from consumers in vulnerable situations – leaving them with nothing.

In June 2015, the NTS Scams Team first discovered that this company was processing cheques for over 50 companies that were suspected of engaging in mass marketing fraud. The team worked with the banks concerned, who took the decision to freeze and close accounts.

The NTS Scams Team continued to build up a profile of the company and its international reach. It was apparent that the company was being used by the majority of the mail scam companies as their preferred money processor of choice. It was money laundering on a large global scale.

In October 2015, the NTS Scams Team highlighted this company at the International Mass Marketing Fraud Working Group meeting in Brussels. Many members of the group were aware of them. On the recommendation of the NTS Scams Team, a subgroup was formed to continue to look at the activity of this company.

The NTS Scams Team continued to gather intelligence, which was shared with the subgroup. As part of Operation Boemerang, a Dutch investigation supported by NTS Scams Team, further accounts were identified. In addition, there was email evidence to show one of the principals of the company was using an aircraft to pick money up in Holland.

On 22 September, in an unprecedented move, the US Treasury Department deemed this company a 'significant transnational criminal organisation' putting it on the same short list as some of the world's most notorious mobsters, drug cartels and murderers.

A staggering quantity of mass mailing fraud has gone through these companies' accounts. One company alone was raking in more than £38 million a year from victims. And it was using this company to process these payments.

To help shield their operations from authorities, fraudsters need a way to process payments that won't easily link them to their scheme or raise red flags. That's because many banks will shut down an account or report them to authorities if they detect suspicious activity, like a high number of small deposits, complaints or refunds.

Criminals responsible for scams instead turn to a payment processor like this one.

American agencies determined that 75 per cent (out of 749) of all cheques sent by one consumer who was repeatedly targeted by criminals responsible for scams sending fraudulent letters were deposited by the named company. This added up to nearly £18,500, which went to at least 50 different mail fraud schemes (involving at least 18 separate companies).

This is just a small fraction of the tens of millions of dollars in scam proceeds that have been deposited by this company.

(Continued)

In declaring this company a transnational criminal group, Treasury Department official John Smith reported all company property or interests subject to US jurisdiction had been blocked, while the Department of Justice conducts searches and proceeds with criminal actions.

It is alleged that this company has facilitated mail fraud for several years allowing consumers in vulnerable situations to be defrauded out of millions (probably billions) of pounds. Preventing this company's operation will cause a huge amount of disruption to the criminals sending fraudulent mail to UK residents.

The NTS Scams Team continues to work with the National Crime Agency and US authorities.

Work with mail providers

The NTS Scams Team works in partnership with mail providers to combat scam mail. The mail comes from abroad via many different avenues and mail providers. This mail is still coming into the system and being delivered to consumers in our local communities.

Recent reviews have enabled mail providers to take a more proactive approach to tackling scam mail, including an industry-wide response to clamp down on scam mail.

An industry-wide Code of Practice has been written and all mail providers have been encouraged to sign up.

The Code of Practice

Companies signing up to the Code of Practice will voluntarily commit to meeting the following obligations:

1. To actively work together, and with law enforcement agencies, to tackle the scourge of scam mail.

2. The proactive sharing of intelligence of confirmed scam mailings and suspected scam mailings.

3. Terminate any mail identified by law enforcement agencies as being used to attempt to scam the recipients.

4. Include anti-scam terms and conditions in contracts.

5. Closer ties with the broader communications, community and law enforcement agencies to prevent scams through letters, electronic communications, telephone calls and other means.

6. Actively work together as an industry to mitigate the risk posed by scam mail and to support initiatives to identify people at risk of criminals responsible for scams. Provide help and support for victims of scams by sharing information received in our enquiries with appropriate partners including: the National Trading Standards Scams Team, law enforcement and other agencies.

The NTS Scams Team currently works with Royal Mail to train postal workers to identify scam mail and those people that are receiving it with a view to getting the right support and intervention.

What next? Prevention and detection of scams in the financial sector

The NTS Scams Team has worked with financial institutions since 2014. The aim is for financial institutions to take a proactive approach in identifying consumers that are victims of fraud, particularly relating to mass marketing fraud and doorstep crime. However, the Data Protection Act 1998 has been used as a barrier to sharing data, often because of fear about the consequences of using data incorrectly.

Legalities

Data Protection Act 1998
The NTS Scams Team would like financial institutions to advise their customers that they are passing their details on to law enforcement (to include the NTS Scams Team) for further advice and guidance. This could be done verbally (for example, when in the branch) or sent in the form of a joint letter from the NTS Scams Team and financial institution. This must be done in an open and transparent way so that the customer knows where their data will be going.

A further consideration is the duty to the public to do so. This is outlined in the court case below.

Public Duty Tournier v National Provincial and Union Bank of England

Bankes Lord Justice said that 'many instances might be given where a bank is justified in disclosing its customers' affairs on the grounds that there is a duty to the public to do so'. However, he did not give any examples. Scrutton Lord Justice said that a bank 'may disclose the customer's account and affairs ... to prevent frauds or crimes' and Atkin Lord Justice considered that the right to disclose exists 'to the extent to which it is reasonably necessary ... to protect the bank, or persons interested, or the public, against fraud or crime'.

The NTS Scams Team believes that it is necessary to share this information to protect the bank and, more specifically, its customers from fraud.

Other considerations include the views expressed by the Financial Services Authority.

> ### 'Banks' defences against investment fraud – Detecting perpetrators and protecting victims', June 2012
>
> *The Financial Services Authority stated in the above paper that they were 'particularly disappointed with the banks' ability to detect where their customers may be complicit in investment fraud. Ongoing monitoring of the customer was often the responsibility of customer-facing staff with many other responsibilities, which often lacked the knowledge to identify investment fraud'.*
>
> *... 'Communication with customers relating to investment fraud also varied; some banks contacted potential victims individually, but others did not'.*

By working in partnership and identifying victims of fraud centrally organisations are enabled to provide victims with the help and support they need at a local level. It also assists the NTS Scams Team in its disruption of the perpetrators of mass marketing fraud and other scams.

REFLECTION 7.1

How can financial institutions work more effectively with trading standards to identify victims of mass marketing fraud and other fraud?

Below are some recommendations from the NTS Scams Team

1. Financial institutions should initially start to identify victims centrally by the number of cheque books they are receiving per year. Based on the NTS Scams Team current statistics the average scam victim is 75. Therefore any consumer over 70 who is receiving at least one cheque book per month would need to have their accounts looked at to see if they are a victim of fraud. This may also help to uncover money mules (i.e. those people inadvertently assisting criminals by dealing with other victims' payments) and victims of other types of fraud.

2. Once victims are identified the following should happen:

   - Joint letter from the NTS Scams Team and financial institution to victim with prevent and protect messages.

   - Names and addresses and a summary of the concern to be passed to the NTS Scams Team. The NTS Scams Team will then pass this information to the local trading standards/police/adult social care so that they can safeguard this individual from further financial abuse and potentially investigate any fraud.

3. We would like financial institutions to exit relationships with companies that we high-light as breaking the law, and thereby contribute to the NTS Scams Team's disruption strategy. Limiting banking facilities in the UK limits the amount of money companies can receive from consumers. The NTS Scams Team aim to provide sufficient evidence for financial institutions to make a decision in this respect.

   - Once a company has been identified as breaking the law, victims who have paid money into those accounts should be identified. This should result in: Joint letter from the NTS Scams Team and financial institution to victim with prevent and pro-tect messages.

   - Names and addresses and a summary of the concern to be passed to the NTS Scams Team. The NTS Scams Team will then pass this information to the local trading standards/police so that they can safeguard this individual from further financial abuse and potentially investigate any fraud.

4. Financial institutions should provide intelligence on suspected scam companies to the NTS Scams Team who can then take action where necessary.

CASE STUDY 7.5

A new inter-agency collaboration

On 10 February 2016 the Joint Fraud Taskforce was launched. It aims to combine the work of law enforcement, government, the banking sector and big business to crack down on fraud. The Taskforce creates a new era of collaboration, resulting in shared intelligence, a unified response and greater awareness of the risk of fraud amongst consumers.

This includes:

- *Improving the law enforcement response – supporting better data collection and analysis at a national level and prioritisation of fraud investigations at a local level.*

- *Understanding the threat – working to identify key priorities for the Taskforce and spot intelligence gaps and vulnerabilities. Fast-tracking intelligence sharing between banks and law enforcement for a more coordinated approach to serious and organised crime gangs.*

- *The role of technology in preventing 'Card Not Present' fraud – the Home Secretary commissioned an industry-led Strategic Action Plan on 'Card Not Present' fraud to tackle systemic vulnerabilities and removing weak links in systems and processes which fraud-sters can exploit.*

- *Funds repatriation for victims – a proof of concept is ongoing to allow for quick tracking of fraudulent transactions making it much easier to freeze and return funds to victims.*

- *Awareness-raising campaign – a very visible, persistent and well-funded fraud preven-tion campaign is needed so we have clear and consistent messaging on fraud. Identifying why victims fall prey to fraud and helping to raise awareness of the steps they can take to protect themselves.*

(Continued)

CASE STUDY *7.5* *(CONT.)*

- *Victims and vulnerability – the Home Secretary is clear that improving the situation for victims and the vulnerable is a priority. This includes more efficient identification of victims and potential victims, including national roll-out of intervention training for bank staff.*

The Victims and Vulnerability or Victims and Susceptibility strand is co-ordinated by the NTS Scams Team and Victim Support Services. This aims to significantly improve the service victims of fraud receive and the protections offered to those who may be more susceptible to becoming a victim.

Objectives of the strand include:

1. **Developing a defined multi-agency response for victims of fraud:** Aims to rectify the inconsistent service fraud victims receive from the different agencies.

2. **National roll-out of the banking protocol:** A branch-based intervention designed to help identify potential victims and, where appropriate, seek quick interventions from the police or trading standards.

3. **Develop and implement a new minimum standard for the treatment of those who are vulnerable to fraud:** Includes encouraging banks to implement a new British Standards Institute (BSI) Public Available Specification (PAS) Standard to better protect customers who may be susceptible to fraud. Consideration will be given to the introduction of a Quality Mark for those financial institutions that meet the PAS, and additional specifications focused on improving the victim's experience.

4. **Improved data sharing between key agencies to better support victims and potential victims:** Financial institutions will be supported to better assist in the identification of victims of fraud.

5. **Introduction of fraud protection measures for bank customers:** Includes –

   - caps on the amount payable to new payees;
   - notification text messages on particular account activity;
   - tailored warning messages;
   - opting out of faster payments.

6. **Consistent approach to victims under Code of Practice for Victims of Crime (2015):** Options include removing inconsistency and greater adoption of the definition within the Code of Practice for Victims of Crime that an individual remains a victim if they have directly suffered harm (including mental or emotional harm) because of a fraud.

This work offers the opportunity to identify victims and provide them with the support and interventions that are needed to prevent further fraud. Joined-up inter-agency working is required to tackle this colossal problem and protect people in our communities, and it is hoped that the Joint Fraud Taskforce will provide a positive way forward.

Conclusion

The NTS Scams Team plays a unique and highly valued role in promoting action against scams (Lonsdale, 2016). Its work is widely respected within the trading standards community and amongst a diverse and growing range of partners. The RAND survey (Lonsdale, 2016) suggests that almost all respondents considered the team was 'effective' in fulfilling its objective of tackling scams, and effective in supporting their work. Local trading standards and other external partners consider that the team is tackling a problem which other agencies have failed to recognise or tackle in the past. The RAND research concludes that the Scams Team appears to be delivering significant added value, securing beneficial outcomes which could not, and would not, be secured in its absence (**http://www.rand.org/pubs/research_reports/RR1510.html**). However, the NTS Scams Team recognises that without the local trading standards services visiting, supporting and intervening with identified victims, the model would fail. The front-line workers within local authorities work relentlessly to support the scam victims in their local areas.

Key learning points

- Trading standards plays a core role in consumer protection and enforcement.
- The National Trading Standards Scams Team is a dedicated team focused on interrupting mass marketing scams and supporting victims.
- The team have identified thousands of scam victims.
- It is estimated that between £5 and £10 billion is lost to mass marketing fraud each year.
- Partnership work between statutory services, voluntary agencies, law enforcement and the financial sector is necessary to provide an effective response to scams and other fraud.

Chapter 8

Doorstep crime: rogue trading and distraction burglary

Tim Day

CHAPTER OUTCOMES

As a result of completing this chapter you will:

- Understand the definitions of doorstep crime.

- Understand the victimology of doorstep criminality and why safeguarding is a key factor in the prevention and reduction of harm.

- Appreciate the scale of doorstep criminality and why it is difficult to assess.

- Understand the enforcement landscape in relation to doorstep crime.

Introduction

In discussing rogue trading and doorstep crime, it is first necessary to define the phenomena. This is complicated by the lack of a definitive definition or Home Office classification for the terms rogue trading and doorstep crime. It is further confused by the use of the term 'rogue trader' to describe both the form of doorstep crime explored within this chapter, and unauthorised investment trading at financial institutions (Day, 2015).

To provide clarity therefore, within this chapter the following definitions are used:

The term **doorstep crime** describes the practice of rogue trading and/or distraction burglary. There is an identified overlap between the two crime types, with offenders known to switch between the methods of offending depending upon the victim, their credulity and the circumstances and situation (Steele *et al.*, 2001; ACTSO, 2015).

Rogue trading

Any incident where an individual, or individuals, targets a consumer, deliberately over-charging for unsatisfactory goods and/or services. This includes charging for unnecessary work, damaging property in order to obtain money or work, charging for work not carried out, leaving work unfinished and intimidating behaviour in order to extort money (ACSTO, 2015).

Distraction burglary is defined by the Home Office as shown in the box below.

Distraction burglary

Any crime where a falsehood, trick or distraction is used on an occupant of a dwelling to gain, or try to gain, access to the premises to commit burglary. It includes cases where the offender first enters the premises and subsequently uses distraction burglary methods in order to remain on the premises and/or gain access to other parts of the premises in order to commit burglary (Home Office, 2004).

Types of offender

Rogue trading doorstep criminals are said to fit within three distinct categories or 'types'.

Types of rogue trading doorstep criminal (ACTSO, 2014)

1. Chancers/apprentices:

Largely opportunistic and sporadic in the extent of their offending, this type of offender often identifies victims through cold-calling as opposed to targeting pre-existing victims. Offenders carry out all types of property maintenance and repairs and often will not confine themselves to one trade area, carrying out anything from cleaning or replacing driveways and block paving, to guttering and roof cleaning or repairs, to tree surgery and gardening/garden clearance, insulation and painting and decorating. They cold call large areas, going door-to-door and will repeatedly victimise consumers where the opportunity presents. The work carried out is routinely unnecessary, of poor quality and over-priced.

(Continued)

(Continued)

2. Legitimate guise:

This type of offender will deliberately ape legitimate business practices, in order to give the operation an air of legitimacy (amongst both their target group and enforcement agencies). This makes it hard to distinguish between the legitimate and illegitimate companies. It will often involve the business being set up as a limited company, with a registered office and company director(s), associated professional websites and advertising through traditional methods. The business will also often be structured as legitimate businesses, with regional sales managers, sales representatives, etc. Such businesses will either offer general property repairs/maintenance, or specialise in a particular trade sector; roof coating or double glazing, for example. Similarly, they may specialise in selling products such as security alarms, mobility aids, adjustable chairs/beds and energy or energy saving devices. These offenders routinely identify customers through the use of mailing lists.

3. Professional offenders/organised crime groups:

These offenders are highly organised, having spent years developing their skills and MO. They operate in gangs, often including associates and family members, and utilise 'casual labour'. This includes the exploited labour of vulnerable individuals such as those who are homeless, unemployed, have alcohol and drug dependencies and immigrants with limited English language skills, especially those who are not legally entitled to work in the country.

They travel widely to commit their offending and use accommodation addresses to give the appearance of a fixed trading entity. Such offenders also utilise traditional methods of advertising, including through their own and other websites, leaflet dropping and posting flyers door-to-door, as well as via approved trader schemes to enhance their professional appearance. They are also known to share information regarding victims and detection methods employed by enforcement agencies, and repeat victimisation over extended periods of time is a common tactic, especially where the victim is vulnerable and affluent. This offender type also makes widespread use of money launderers to conceal and clean their criminal proceeds, including using female family members and casual acquaintances who take a cut for processing cheques and accepting money transfers to their accounts.

Doorstep crime offenders

Whilst doorstep crime is acquisitive crime, and the motive is predominantly one of financial gain, nonetheless there is within some offending groups also an element of status and kudos in what is perceived as the skillful manipulation of victims to enable successful offending, with offenders taking considerable pride in their ability to deceive their victims (Steele *et al.*, 2001; Phillips, 2016). They are known to travel widely to commit their crimes (Barratt, 2012), operating regionally, nationally and even internationally (Europol, 2011), attempting by doing so to frustrate enforcement agencies' abilities to apprehend them or identify the full extent of their offending. Some perpetrators are known to carry out hundreds of such offences throughout their career and often have multiple previous convictions for the same or similar offences, such as burglary, theft and fraud. This is equally true of distraction burglary as it is of rogue trading, though it is believed rogue trading is both more prevalent and more lucrative for the perpetrators (Steele *et al.*, 2001; Day, 2015).

Doorstep criminals rationalise their offending such that, despite wider society finding their actions abhorrent, they believe they are not doing wrong or visiting harm upon their victims (Steele *et al.*, 2001; Phillips, 2016). Convicted doorstep criminals variously describe, for example, that their victims do not need the money whereas they do; that their victims are greedy, trying to get a good deal for themselves and so deserve their fate; and that they themselves were victimised by enforcement agencies, as others do far worse without being convicted. Rogue traders are also known to exploit lonely older adults by grooming them to facilitate repeat victimisation (an MO largely unavailable in distraction burglary, where avoidance of detection can rely solely upon the victim not being able to recognise the offender), and again, perpetrators rationalise this by claiming to benefit the victim, making them happy via their social contact.

Victimology

Distraction burglary

The average age of distraction burglary victims is 77 years old, 77 per cent of victims are female, and 74 per cent live alone, with 23 per cent reporting that they had no one to call on in times of adversity (Barratt, 2012).

Rogue trading

65 per cent of victims are aged 75 years old and over, with 20 per cent being aged between 80 and 85 years old. 54 per cent of victims are female, and 57 per cent live alone (ACTSO, 2015).

REFLECTION *8.1*

Given the offender and victim profiles of doorstep crime, which agencies do you think have a role to play in safeguarding, enforcement and crime prevention? And what might that role include?

Is their role the same for distraction burglary as it is for rogue trading, or are there differences?

Police, trading standards, safeguarding and adult social care all have a key role to play in doorstep crime enforcement and safeguarding. The enforcement and safeguarding aspects should be interconnected and both should consider the needs of the victim as paramount. For example, with vulnerable victims the video recording and use of special measures to achieve best evidence can alleviate some of the anxiety of giving evidence and involvement with the criminal justice system as much as it can assist the criminal investigation itself. Think about the nature of the relationship between these agencies in your area, and what each of the agencies might contribute. How might this be improved or strengthened in the future?

The local community and third sector agencies can also play an important part in crime prevention, safeguarding and reporting of doorstep crime. For instance, given the propensity of offenders to target properties where there are visible signs of vulnerability, such as an unkempt garden, safeguarding agencies may attempt to commission a voluntary organisation to assist with tidying and garden maintenance as a crime prevention measure.

Effective and ongoing communication between agencies is important so that each can reinforce the messages of their partner agencies, as well as their own. This is as important for distraction burglary as it is for rogue trading. Whilst trading standards traditionally do not become involved in the investigation of distraction burglary, they may still have intelligence or information that could be valuable to police and so liaison between the agencies on these cases should be considered best practice. Whilst the role of each of the agencies may differ slightly according to the specific crime type, the aims of the agencies should be the same. These will involve bringing the offender to justice and/or securing justice for the victim, minimising the harm and safeguarding the victim from the effects of the incident, as well as reducing the prospect of future victimisation.

The victim profile for distraction burglary and rogue trading is similar, and it is especially valuable information to those agencies responsible for, or involved with, the safeguarding of adults at risk of abuse and neglect because of the overlap with their client group. The discussion that follows further explores the stark similarities between doorstep crime victims and adult safeguarding clients.

In part the victim profile for doorstep crime can be ascribed to the deliberate targeting of older adults at risk of neglect and abuse by the perpetrators, because of their belief that older and vulnerable persons are more likely to be persuaded, and less likely to be able to identify them, or want to go through the criminal justice process.

For older adults with cognitive impairments, such as those experiencing dementia, it may be more difficult to assess the motivation of a doorstep criminal, leaving them more susceptible to victimisation. Moreover, those older adults experiencing loneliness are more likely to engage with cold callers, making them perhaps more likely to fall victim as a result (Lee and Geistfeld, 1999). Clearly this will be compounded by the deliberate targeting of these groups by determined criminals looking to financially exploit them, a fact of concern to those with cognitive impairment or decline (and their carers), given that 15 per cent of carers believe the person to whom they give care has been targeted by organised criminals (Alzheimer's Society, 2011).

Chapters 4 and 5 provide further discussion of the relationship between loneliness, social isolation and dementia with all forms of scamming.

However, given that most offences occur within working hours, it might also be that those who are retired and not at work may be more exposed to approaches by the offenders, simply by virtue of their presence in the home during the time when offending occurs, rather than their being more receptive to cold callers per se.

Doorstep criminals are known to search for visible indicators of potential vulnerability when offending and this is perhaps supported by the fact that 43 per cent of rogue trader victims had a handrail/grab rail, ramp to their door, or a key safe for use by carers, and 28 per cent had a neglected garden. Again, this is an important consideration for those involved with safeguarding and adult social care, because the very steps which might be employed to assist an individual with reduced mobility might result in an increased likelihood of their being targeted by doorstep criminals. A more holistic approach may therefore benefit the individual, with those responsible for safeguarding being cognisant not just of the health and mobility needs, but also of the potential for financial abuse. With the introduction of the Care Act 2014, this is all the more so, and mitigating measures might also need to be introduced, alongside mobility aids. Such measures might include CCTV cameras being installed at the property to provide a visual deterrent and a means of evidential capture; the possible introduction of a Lasting Power of Attorney, where appropriate; and working in partnership with financial institutions to request an alert and postponement on any large or unusual activity on their bank account, so that it can be verified with a trusted contact.

Reported health issues of rogue trader victims

- *63 per cent had a physical impairment, for example mobility issues.*
- *38 per cent of victims have falls, with 23 per cent of those being unable to get themselves up after having a fall.*
- *43.5 per cent had a longstanding illness such as cancer, diabetes or heart disease.*
- *39 per cent had sensory impairment.*
- *13 per cent had a mental health condition such as depression.*
- *13 per cent had a cognitive impairment such as dementia.*
- *26 per cent said they, or those close to them, were concerned about their memories.*
- *Over 40 per cent of victims take four or more medications a day.*

(ACTSO, 2015)

In addition to the health issues reported above, victims also experienced difficulty in completing household tasks, with at least 1 in 5 unable to manage their shopping, clean their home, or get to and from medical appointments.

Despite the picture painted by the health issues experienced by victims of rogue trading, and the difficulty they report experiencing undertaking chores, it is worthy of note that only 14 per cent had some form of formal care provision. With the Care Act 2014 placing a statutory obligation upon local authorities to protect those at risk of financial abuse, these figures speak of a need for greater engagement by, and with, adult social care services.

Social care is a key agency in respect of the safeguarding of victims of distraction burglary too, with one study indicating that up to 80 per cent of victims were already known to social care at the point of victimisation (Thornton *et al.*, 2006).

Loneliness and social isolation

Loneliness and social isolation seem to play a role in rogue trader victimisation, as they do with other forms of scamming as discussed in Chapter 3. This role is particularly seen in regard to repeat victimisation. It has been explained previously that some offenders will groom vulnerable individuals, exploiting loneliness, often ruthlessly until all their money has been defrauded. It has also been noted how lonely older adults are more likely to engage with doorstep traders and cold callers. It is of little surprise then that 34 per cent of victims of rogue trading reported that they had experienced bereavement in the past 2 years, 17 per cent that they left their home once a week or less and that 41 per cent said they felt lonely, with 26 per cent feeling lonely every day.

Grooming and repeat victimisation

What I really like is people who live on their own and have no-one to confide in. We can just keep going back to their house, talking to them and making them happy and pretending to do a bit of work. We can take thousands off them in a matter of weeks without anyone finding out and stopping us.

Doorstep crime convict (Steele et al., 2001, p61)

In some instances the exploitation does not end when the victim can no longer afford to pay any money, with offenders sometimes known to persuade victims to transfer ownership of their homes, in lieu of further payment (see for instance *R v Tomney* [2012] EWCA Crim 2545).

REFLECTION *8.2*

What effect might the removal of a financially abusive social contact have for a lonely victim? And how could this be mitigated?

Removal of a financially abusive social contact might abruptly force the victim to confront the fact they are being exploited for financial gain, by someone whom they considered a friend. The effects of this sudden realisation of victimisation can be devastating, shattering victims' perception of their world and their own self-image, and leading to a rapid decline in physical and mental health. Moreover, the removal of the contact in itself is likely to aggravate the victim's loneliness, further negatively affecting their health, well-being and state of mind. Additionally, the 'void' left by the removal of the offender may lead to the victim being more likely to be repeat victimised; their loneliness may result in them being more receptive to approaches by others intent on defrauding them. These effects can be mitigated through a number of ways:

- The empathetic and sympathetic involvement of law enforcement agencies, and communication of the situation to the victim.

- The involvement of agencies over a period of time, rather than delivering the news and ending their involvement all at once.

- The replacement of the financially abusive social contact with a more healthy relationship, such as that of a befriender or the introduction to a local community group, etc.

- The involvement of safeguarding agencies to ensure the individual's needs are understood and met and that entitlement to support is identified and communicated.

- The involvement, with consent, of a trusted friend or family member, where possible and appropriate. Even facilitating a hobby or 'purpose' of the victim can reduce the impact and boost resilience.

Impact of doorstep crime

Both distraction burglary and rogue trading have a considerable impact on their victims. The boxes below summarise the reported effects.

Distraction burglary

40 per cent of victims reported a change in their quality of life (Barratt, 2012).

10 per cent had unexplained admissions to hospital within three months of the burglary (Thornton et al., 2006).

In the two years following a distraction burglary, victims are almost 2.5 times more likely to be in residential care or to have died than their non-victim peers (Donaldson, 2003).

Repeat victims are likely to suffer from post-traumatic stress disorder (Barratt, 2012).

Rogue trading

23 per cent of victims reported an impact on their health.

38 per cent said it reduced their confidence generally and 26 per cent that it left them feeling down or depressed.

12 per cent were left feeling afraid in their own homes and 13 per cent felt more afraid of crime as a result of the incident.

(ACTSO, 2015)

Whilst these figures give a picture of the impact of doorstep crime, it is difficult to generalise too widely, as impact is dependent on so many factors, and varies because victims are all individuals rather than a homogenous group (Gorden and Buchanan, 2013).

Factors that can affect the victim impact of doorstep crime

- *The level of financial loss, particularly as a proportion of a victim's wealth (e.g. the loss of £20,000 may be less harmful to someone with hundreds of thousands of pounds than the loss of £500 for someone already experiencing poverty).*

- *The level of awareness of having been victimised (those unaware of the criminality will be, aside from the financial loss, largely unaffected).*

- *Longevity of victimisation (repeat victimisation is likely to have a greater impact than a one-off incident – both financially and in terms of the victims' health and well-being).*

- *Loss of items of sentimental value (may have a greater impact than the loss of money alone).*

- *Availability of support networks (socially isolated and lonely victims may feel the impact more acutely).*

- *Victims' personal resilience (some may feel the impact more greatly than others).*

- *Enforcement response (those who are dissatisfied with the enforcement response they receive suffer greater anxiety, and for longer, than those who are provided a response deemed satisfactory).*

Assessing the extent of doorstep crime

Accurately assessing the scale of doorstep crime is all but impossible. Whilst it is possible with ease to measure levels of recorded distraction burglaries (at least since the introduction of a definition and Home Office crime code for the criminality in 2003), there is a recognised difficulty whereby a proportion of incidents go unreported. The true scale of the criminality is therefore largely unknown.

Reasons for under-reporting

- *Fear of repercussions from offenders or their associates.*
- *Fear of getting involved in the criminal justice system/process.*
- *Fear of loss of their independence.*
- *Lack of mental capacity.*
- *Not understanding/accepting they are a victim.*
- *Social isolation and loneliness.*
- *Embarrassment/self-blame.*
- *Considering it is inappropriate to report.*
- *Believing it is futile to report.*
- *Not knowing who to report to.*
- *Generational issues.*
- *Wanting to ignore the incident or forget about it.*

(ACTSO, 2014)

REFLECTION 8.3

What results may these barriers to reporting have for doorstep crime victims?

All of the barriers listed above result in the victim lacking support from the agencies which are responsible for safeguarding victims of crime and vulnerable older adults. This means, in addition to the inability to prosecute the offender (or the potential of compensation for the victim), there are no opportunities for crime prevention messages to be imparted, or target hardening initiatives to be put in place. Unfortunately this also means that, since offenders are known to share information about vulnerable victims, the potential for repeat victimisation is very real.

Rogue trading, together with the same problems with (and reasons for) under-reporting as distraction burglary (see box above), also suffers from myriad other difficulties when trying to gauge its prevalence. The additional difficulties are briefly explored below.

Lack of definition

The lack of a definitive definition, as outlined at the beginning of the chapter, means that it is unclear at times whether and in what circumstances an incident of rogue trading is simply a civil law contractual dispute between a consumer and an otherwise legitimate trader, a criminal incident (but outside the scope of what can be termed rogue trading), or a criminal incident within the realm of what can be considered to be rogue trading or doorstep crime. This lack of clarity is an issue for both consumers (including victims) and enforcement agencies, and the results are two-pronged. First, it can result in victims wrongly dismissing the incident without reporting it, and second it may also lead to enforcement agencies wrongly classifying cases which *are* reported to them as civil law issues, without thoroughly investigating or properly recording them as a crime (Day, 2015).

Multiple reporting routes for rogue trading

Unlike distraction burglary, which is undisputedly the domain of the police to investigate, rogue trading is investigated and dealt with by both police and local authorities, and each agency has its own (and more than one) route to reporting an incident.

Examples of reporting routes for rogue trading

- *Police*
  - o *local police (e.g. report via 101 or 999)*
  - o *national police (e.g. report via Action Fraud)*
- *Local authority*
  - o *local trading standards (e.g. report directly in to local trading standards)*
  - o *national consumer advice line (e.g. report via Cit A consumer helpline)*

The effect of the multiple reporting routes is that the national picture of the extent of rogue trading is fragmented, with each agency only privy to and responsible for a particular fraction of the overall recording.

Lack of retrievability of reports of rogue trading

The difficulties outlined above are further compounded by the lack of a crime code, or flag, for rogue trading, resulting in a lack of retrievability of those incidents that have been reported and recorded by police (whether that is each individual force area, or Action Fraud).

Table 8.1 Comparison of distraction burglary and rogue trading records from the Thames Valley Police crime recording database (June, July and August 2013)

	Distraction burglary	Rogue trading
Number of incidents	16	23
Number of attempts	5 unsuccessful distraction burglary attempts.	5 potential unsuccessful rogue trading attempts (involving the damage of roof tiles and guttering, recorded as criminal damage).
Number of crime categories necessary to search	2	11
Number of these crime categories in which attempts or incidents occurred	2	6
Number of records that required analysis	21	3798

(Day, 2015)

Table 8.1 highlights the difficulties in retrieval experienced as a result of the lack of a crime code, or flag, using just 3 months of crime records from one police force.

As can be seen the need to manually trawl 3798 police records in order to identify just 23 completed incidents and five attempted incidents of rogue trading means that in practice, with the bigger dataset necessary to understand the national picture, or over a longer timeframe, the task is rendered impossible.

Obfuscating the situation still further, there is little standardisation amongst trading standards or local authorities in terms of the recording of rogue trading, making accurate retrieval of the information held by these agencies problematic as well. Moreover, because of limitations in the databases and recording mechanisms utilised by local authorities, even where an incident is recorded, if further investigation identifies multiple victims and additional financial detriment, these will often go unrecorded (ACTSO, 2015). Again this results in an under-estimate of the extent of rogue trading and makes accurately gauging the size and scale of the problem notoriously difficult.

Estimates of the extent of doorstep crime

Notwithstanding the issues identified above, it is nonetheless useful to contextualise the potential scale of the criminality by attempting to quantify the extent of doorstep crime as accurately as possible.

Distraction burglary

Table 8.2 Distraction burglary offences (England and Wales) (Statistics from Operation Liberal, 2014)

Financial year	Number recorded	Number detected	Percentage detected
2006–2007	12,750	1,358	10.65
2007–2008	10,635	961	9.04
2008–2009	9,090	1,192	13.11
2009–2010	7,657	1,064	13.9
2010–2011	6,024	1,132	18.79
2011–2012	4,831	1,010	21.00
2012–2013	3,562	655	18.00
2013–2014	3,068	–	–

(Day, 2015)

As Table 8.2 shows, the latest figures indicate just over 3000 recorded incidents of distraction burglary in England and Wales. It is also of note there has been a year-on-year decrease in levels of recorded distraction burglary since the introduction of the definition and crime code in 2003, with an overall reduction of 75 per cent.

Rogue trading

Using the average number of incidents recorded per local authority area in 2013–2014 and 2014–2015 (ACTSO, 2015), it was possible to estimate the total number of reports of rogue trading to trading standards. Table 8.3 shows the results.

It is vital to recognise that the figure in the table is for local authorities only and takes no account of police or Action Fraud data (the retrieval of police data proved impossible due to the lack of a crime code or flag by which to identify rogue trading incidents). It is therefore a considerable under-estimate of the scale of rogue trading. Irrespective of this, it is still possible to compare the levels of incidents with those of distraction burglary and posit that rogue trading is far more prevalent than distraction burglary. Indeed, one school of thought is that, as levels of distraction burglary have decreased, there may have been a corresponding increase in levels of rogue trading, particularly given the identified overlap between the offences by the

Table 8.3 Estimated prevalence of rogue trading incidents reported to local authorities

Financial year	Estimated number of reports received by trading standards
2013–2014	16,849
2014–2015	17,264

perpetrators (Day, 2015). The increase in reports received by trading standards over the two years studied may tend to support this claim. In this case the attention given to distraction burglary may unwittingly have steered offenders to the (already more lucrative) crime of rogue trading.

Estimates of reporting rates of rogue trading incidents by trading standards suggest that *only between 1 per cent and 10 per cent are ever reported*. This would mean anywhere *between 172,640 and 1,726,400 incidents of rogue trading* occurred during 2014–2015. Even a similar rate of reporting for *distraction burglary* would mean *between 30,600 and 306,000 incidents*; far fewer than estimates for rogue trading.

Financial loss from doorstep crime

As with estimates of prevalence and impact, estimates of financial harm resulting from doorstep crime are also difficult, and again, the difficulties are compounded for rogue trading by the lack of crime code or flag by which to identify and retrieve incidents from police records.

However, despite lacking definitive figures, exploration of the financial detriment caused as a result of doorstep crime is important. Such estimates may enable future comparison with other acquisitive crime types traditionally seen as higher priority by police (such as domestic burglary and thefts from vehicles), and could result in evidence based resource decisions as to the relative harm and financial cost to victims.

Distraction burglary

> *In 2011 the average loss, per victim, to distraction burglary was calculated as £648.36 (Operation Liberal, n.d.).*

The actual amounts lost as a result of distraction burglary vary greatly. For example, previously in the Metropolitan Police area, one victim had £100,000 stolen from under a bed (Home Office, 2003).

Rogue trading

Whilst having regard to the under-reporting and under-recording of financial detriment alluded to earlier, as a result of the limitations of local authority incident recording databases, the figure below gives an idea, albeit a likely under-estimate, of the detriment caused by rogue trading.

> *In 2014–2015 the average loss, per victim, to rogue trading from reports to trading standards was calculated as £1280 (ACTSO, 2015).*

> *The **average loss**, per victim, to **rogue trading** from a sample of reports to Action Fraud was calculated as £3500 (ACTSO, 2015).*

The variance of losses to rogue trading are also considerable with some perpetrators, as raised earlier, known to have persuaded victims to transfer ownership of their homes in lieu of payment for poor quality, unnecessary work (EWCA Crim. 2545, 2012). Losses of approaching £1,000,000 have also been discovered (Colley, 2016).

A comparison of the average losses in rogue trading and distraction burglary highlights the greater financial detriment in rogue trading cases (£648 as opposed to £1200, or £3500). This is somewhat intuitive as distraction burglars are only able to take that which is kept or concealed in the home, whereas if a rogue trader is able to convince a victim of the need to pay, they can potentially gain access to whatever the victim has within their bank account.

In addition, calculations of loss fail to take account of the additional costs associated with rogue trading, whereby it is often necessary for victims to commission legitimate traders to rectify poorly completed work, or criminal damage caused by the criminals. Quite apart from the financial loss, the anxiety for victims of having to commission further work to their properties, having just been defrauded as a result of previous work, is easy to imagine.

The greater average loss identified from Action Fraud reports may be reflective of the fact that the police is the agency generally regarded as the first port-of-call for crime reporting, especially where they believe the criminality is serious. Trading standards does not have the same profile as a criminal law enforcement agency and the level of criminality reported to local authorities and trading standards therefore may be at the lower end of the spectrum (Day, 2015).

CASE STUDY *8.1*

Rogue trader

A complaint came via the National Consumer Helpline to trading standards. The complaint related to roofing work to a detached property just outside a medium-sized town.

The older couple who lived at the address had been cold-called by a roofing company, the representatives of which told them that they were working locally when they noticed some repairs were needed to the ridge tiles of the property.

The company went on to complete some repointing, before discovering further work was necessary to the roof, and over the course of 2 days carried out work in the loft of the property to strengthen the roof to stop it from collapsing. The older couple were then told the loft had been sprayed with a fungicide upon completion and that they should not go in it for several days as a result. It wasn't until the couple's son visited and looked into the loft that the report was made, as he was suspicious about the work which had been completed.

No paper work, cancellation notice, contract or receipt was given to the consumer.

On interviewing the victims they further explained that the company had a liveried van and uniforms and both victims provided a detailed description of one of the offenders, the 'foreman', who was distinctive and they both believed they would recognise him if they saw him again.

The victims described how they had been given the bank details for the transfer of the money, £8500, for the work to their roof (work which was later deemed to have been unnecessary and of nil value by a surveyor). They described how they were then told to make an additional payment of £4000, but that they avoided paying this only as they had no money left with which to pay. Even then the foreman put pressure on them to try to get them to obtain a loan.

The description given matched that of a man already on police bail for another rogue trader case, with a similar MO. Upon answering bail for that incident the man was further arrested for the incident described above and interviewed under caution. He answered no comment to any and all questions put to him and declined to take part in a Video Identification Parade Electronic Recording (VIPER) procedure. As he had been arrested, however, his custody photograph was used in a VIPER procedure, without his consent. The VIPER procedure resulted in the elderly couple both, independently, identifying the suspect as the perpetrator who had acted as the foreman.

The bank details and the fact money from a suspected fraud had been transferred to the account was also sufficient for an Accredited Financial Investigator to obtain a Production Order on the account in question. This led to proof that the £8500 paid by the victims had been received into the account, and the discovery of a further victim, who had paid £11,750 into the same account.

The other victim was traced; he was an older male, living alone, who had cancer. The description he gave of the man in charge again matched that of the suspect identified by the other victims in the VIPER procedure. The victim described how he was cold called and convinced of the need for roofing work, and that the work and the cost had soon spiralled out of his control. He felt that the man had stolen from him, but he did not report the incident. The victim described how he would return from hospital from appointments for his cancer treatment only to be greeted by the man demanding further money for work he claimed to have undertaken whilst the victim was undergoing treatment. He wasn't given any information about cancellation rights, nor provided a contract or any receipts.

Again, an expert witness was commissioned to assess the work and he judged it to be minimal, and of such poor quality as to have zero value.

The victim was able to provide a piece of paper which the man had given to him, on which he had written the bank details to which the money should be paid. This piece of paper was sent for forensic examination and was found to have on it the fingerprints of the man arrested for the other incident, who had been identified by the victims in the VIPER procedure.

The suspect was interviewed again in relation to the further evidence regarding both offences and again chose to give no comment throughout.

(Continued)

Ultimately the suspect pleaded guilty to fraud and money laundering offences in relation to the above incidents, in the face of overwhelming evidence. In summing up the judge described it as a despicable, pre-planned and relatively sophisticated crime, preying on the sick and elderly before sentencing the offender to 30 months imprisonment, which was reduced to 20 months as a result of the early guilty plea.

The enforcement landscape

As discussed, whilst distraction burglary is investigated by police, responsibility for the enforcement of rogue trading does not rest solely with the police. Local authority trading standards departments play a key role in the enforcement of rogue trading.

The enforcement response each agency provides rogue trading is examined below.

Police

It is clear that there is something of a dissonance between the stated priorities of police forces and the actions they are taking in respect of rogue trading when the victimology is borne in mind. Despite 95 per cent stating protecting the vulnerable is a priority within their Crime Plan or Police and Crime Commissioner (PCC) strategy, the majority of forces (62 per cent) are unable to analyse the criminality, or monitor or report on the levels of rogue trading within their force area. Moreover only 14 per cent of forces stated they give high priority to doorstep crime, whereas 32 per cent acknowledged they assign it a low priority, and that they did not investigate incidents to the same standard as other crimes. This is also despite 32 per cent of forces stating they have Organised Crime Groups scored in relation to doorstep crime (ACTSO, 2015) (and tackling organised crime is also a featured priority within many forces' Crime Plans or PCC strategies).

Reasons for police not allocating a higher priority to doorstep crime

Limited resources 72 per cent

Lack of awareness of doorstep crime 33 per cent

Lack of training 17 per cent

Lack of skills 17 per cent

Lack of understanding 22 per cent

The absence of a national reporting requirement for rogue trading 22 per cent

Trading standards

There is seemingly a similar discord between the priority trading standards state they provide rogue trading, and the resources they actually put towards it as there is with the police response when juxtaposing their response with their priority areas.

For example, even though 62 per cent of local authorities stated they give a high priority to enforcement, 60 per cent stated they are spending 10 per cent or less of their budget on tackling rogue trading.

The effectiveness of the investigations and enforcement action undertaken by trading standards is put into question by findings which show that the average number of rogue trader prosecutions per authority is just under 1 per year (0.95) in 2014–2015, with only marginally higher the previous year (1.07). Additionally, only 15 per cent of all local authorities had taken two or more prosecutions, which was itself an increase on the previous year where only 13 per cent achieved two or more prosecutions.

The resource spent on trading standards is a useful counterpoint when gauging the effectiveness of enforcement in doorstep crime. Total spend has reduced from £213 million nationally in 2009, to just £124 million in 2015, with five services receiving a budget of less than £200,000 (Silvester, 2016). The real-world impact of this is illustrated by a 23 per cent reduction in those placing high priority on doorstep crime enforcement, going from 80 per cent in 2013–2014, to 62 per cent in 2014–2015, with 96 per cent of authorities stating they would assign rogue trader enforcement work a high priority if resources allowed.

The response doorstep crime is currently receiving is below that which victims should be able to expect, and with there being no signs of an increase in budget for public services, it is more important than ever to find ways of working which increase effectiveness. A closer partnership between the police and trading standards would be mutually beneficial. It would provide a welcome increase in the understanding, training and skills of the police in dealing with rogue trading. It would also enable trading standards to access investigative and forensic tools which are currently widely unavailable to them, such as fingerprinting and DNA analysis, arrest of suspects and imposition of bail conditions.

A closer partnership between enforcement agencies and adult social care services is also much needed. The demography and social situation of the majority of victims, and the harm the removal of a financially abusive 'friend' can cause, as well as the potential complexity of the myriad needs of vulnerable victims, makes contact with social care important. The availability and eligibility criteria for services and benefits are complex and subject to change, and it is only professionals within the area that can be familiar with them. Additionally, the harm that loneliness and social isolation can cause (now understood to be akin to obesity and substance abuse (Holt-Lunstad *et al.*, 2015)), and the increased likelihood of those that are lonely to become victims (and repeat victims), means that engagement with third sector organisations is also important.

The adoption of a crime flag by which to identify incidents of rogue trading would enable better monitoring and scrutiny of crime rates and geographical offending patterns, as well as effective assessment of crime reduction initiatives and performance management of rogue trader cases. This, in turn, may benefit victims through more effective outcomes in terms of prosecution and possible proceeds of crime compensation awards, and through a greater satisfaction of the enforcement response, mitigating, rather than exacerbating, the harm of the crime.

Practical steps for rogue trader investigations

Rogue trader investigations can be viewed in terms of a number of different stages:

1. Formation of robust frameworks and inter-agency response and protocols

The success or otherwise of an investigation is frequently determined by the speed with which enforcers can respond to the incident and comprehensive rogue trader investigations rely on a network of agencies complementing each other's work. Outcomes depend heavily on the strength of pre-existing partnerships based on agreed and clearly communicated response levels. As such, implementing systematic ways of working that facilitate quick responses (such as a rapid response team, the presence of police on scene and the real-time sharing of intelligence and safeguarding issues) are essential.

2. Initial incident response

The initial investigation response includes attending to the immediate needs of the victim and the securing of evidence. It is paramount to consider the needs and wishes of the victims throughout the investigation.

The aim must be to minimise and mitigate any harm the incident has caused, and to avoid revictimisation through the investigative process.

To make this as effective as possible, it is best to take a partnership approach to minimising the harm to the victim, including using social care, safeguarding and third sector professionals and maximising enforcement opportunities through work with the police.

3. Incident follow-up and attending to longer term victim needs

These steps tend to be given lower priority than the initial incident response, but are key to both ensuring the well-being of the victim and the continued feasibility of enforcement action. It is important to consider the needs and wishes of the victims throughout the investigation. Enabling the victim access to the support they need to rebuild their resilience and confidence to continue to live independently is an important aim in itself, but it will often also have the added effect of ensuring they also feel better equipped to support legal action.

Some of the practical steps to consider in the *initial incident response* and the *incident follow-up* stages are summarised below.

Initial incident response

- *Where a suspect is present when a rogue trading incident is reported, a real-time intervention offers the most likely opportunity to halt any (or prevent any further) financial loss, confirm the identity of (and apprehend) the suspect.*

  - o *Quick-response teams, and effective partnership work with the local police (or a Memorandum of Understanding with the local police force) regarding attendance, and where possible arrest, at such incidents is invaluable.*

  - o *This will also enable police to undertake searches of suspects and vehicles on scene, under PACE, potentially uncovering further evidence either related to the offence in question, or potentially other incidents where similar offences have taken place. This might include mobile phones that can be forensically examined, satellite navigation systems containing previous destinations, flyers or leaflets with incorrect addresses, and paper work from other offence locations, etc. It might also enable any subcontractors to be spoken with and offer the opportunity of intelligence gathering and referrals in connection with potentially exploited workers.*

- *Once a suspect has been arrested it will also enable the imposition of conditions on suspects whilst they are on police bail during the course of any subsequent investigation, such as not to return to the address/contact the victim, etc.*

- *Victim care is a key consideration. Does the victim have a relative/friend that can offer support? Do they have a carer, or involvement with adult social care services? Should they be alerted? And might they be able to offer advice regarding the victim and their needs? If the victim does not already have contact with adult social care, might they benefit from/consent to a referral to a safeguarding agency?*

  - o *Consider whether the victim/witnesses, etc. might qualify as vulnerable or intimidated witnesses as defined in the Youth Justice and Criminal Evidence Act 1999, and whether they and their evidence might benefit from an application for special measures.*

  - o *This would include if the individual would find it easier to give a statement via a recorded interview rather than a written statement.*

- *When getting descriptions of suspects, remember the identification guidelines in* R v Turnbull *[1976], and the mnemonic ADVOKATE:*

  A – amount of time the witness saw the suspect.

  D – distance between the witness and suspect.

  V – visibility at the time of the sighting.

  O – obstructions to the sighting.

  K – whether the suspect is known to the witness.

  A – any particular reason that the witness remembers the suspect, or the incident.

(Continued)

137

(Continued)

T – the time elapsed since the incident.

E – bear in mind any errors in the description given by the witness as compared with the actual appearance.

- *Where the suspect is unknown, consider any potential forensic opportunities – are there items at the offence location that could contain fingerprints, such as tools, materials or contracts/receipts, etc.? Or cigarette butts, or cups which suspects have used which might be used for DNA analysis? Work with police to ensure access to such forensic investigation.*

- *Where identification of a suspect is in issue, but the victim believes they would recognise the offender, consider the use of a video identification parade (VIPER) and utilise the police to facilitate the process.*

- *Verify details provided on any contracts/invoices/cancellation forms, etc.; if the address is false or the suspect is not based there, this could give rise to offences such as a Regulation 19 Consumer Contracts (Information, Cancellation and Additional Charges) Regulations 2013 offence (even where the information about the exercise of the right to cancel the contract is otherwise correct), a Regulation 10 Consumer Protection from Unfair Trading Regulations 2008 offence, or even a Section 3 Fraud Act 2006 offence, if the suspect knew of the need for the correct address but deliberately omitted it anyway.*

- *Investigate any paper work left with the victim – is anything seemingly unnecessary/not carried out/grossly overpriced?*

Incident follow-up and longer-term victim needs

- *Consider commissioning an expert witness to provide an opinion on the necessity, quality and value of any works undertaken/quoted and any claims the suspect has made.*

- *Conduct house to house enquiries – this may uncover further victims and/or witnesses, as well as additional suspects and/or descriptions. It may also reveal additional evidence such as homeowner's CCTV footage of suspects/vehicles, etc.*

- *Run any information gathered about any suspect vehicles, nominals, business names and contact details through intelligence databases (both trading standards and police), to see whether further information (or offending, potentially) can be discovered.*

- *Where any vehicle registration details have been gleaned, share these with the police and use Automatic Number Plate Recognition (ANPR) cameras to see whether suspects' journeys can be tracked and suspects identified.*

- Utilise a financial investigator to examine any money transfers or electronic payments, where those payments are believed to be proceeds of crime. The use of money laundering and the Proceeds of Crime Act 2002 potentially provides an additional punishment for offenders, and conversely an additional benefit to victims, through compensation orders whereby offenders repay the victims.

- Keep the victim informed as to the progress of the case, and communicate any significant dates and developments (ensuring for vulnerable or intimidated witnesses that this is done in accordance with the statutory timescales set out in the Youth Justice and Criminal Evidence Act 1999).

- Ensure the victim is made aware of any entitlement to support (for example respite care, if they are acting as a carer) and welfare (such as carers' allowance, council tax reduction if they live alone, etc.) for which they might qualify. Liaise with adult social care.

- Consider whether social isolation and/or loneliness might have contributed to the incident, and whether facilitating social interaction based on the hobbies and wishes of the victim might be of benefit not just for crime prevention, but for health and well-being too.

- Carry out a home safety check to see whether any other actions are necessary, such as the installation of smoke alarms, front door chains, etc.

- Would the victim benefit from a memory assessment by their GP, or a memory clinic?

- Consider whether any other crime prevention and/or harm reduction initiatives might help reassure the victim, for example CCTV cameras installed at the property, no cold-calling door stickers, a 'nominated neighbour' that can help, etc. and whether this can be facilitated.

- Would the victim benefit from measures their financial institution might be able to implement, such as a delay on large or unusual transfers of monies, to enable them to verify the transaction is genuine?

- Has the victim got reliable support, and would they consider a Lasting Power of Attorney to be of benefit?

Key learning points

- Doorstep crime is perpetrated predominantly by organised and professional offenders, and is most often targeted against older and vulnerable adults, particularly those who are lonely.

- The cost of doorstep crime, both in financial terms and in terms of the health and well-being of the victim, can be devastating.

- Accurately assessing the extent of doorstep crime is all but impossible because of numerous factors: the low levels of reporting, the lack of a definition, crime code or flag by which to identify incidents of rogue trading, and the fact that reporting can be via several sources.

- Rogue trading is the form of doorstep crime that is both more common and more financially detrimental to victims than distraction burglary.

- Repeat victimisation and grooming of victims is not uncommon in rogue trading cases, especially amongst the lonely and socially isolated.

- The enforcement response to rogue trading currently lacks effectiveness and falls short of that required.

- Closer partnership working is required across agencies (law enforcement, safeguarding, adult social care, public health, third sector and community groups) to improve the response given to victims and increase the effectiveness of enforcement action in cases of rogue trading.

- A definitive definition and a crime flag by which to identify incidents of rogue trading within police databases would be beneficial to the gathering and retrieval of intelligence, an evidence base on the criminality and the performance management and effectiveness of investigations.

Appendix

The language of scammers

Elisabeth Carter

The final, definitive version of this paper has been published in Crime, Media, Culture: An International Journal 11, 2/2015 by SAGE Publications Ltd, All rights reserved.

Scammers use specific methods of communication to give scams legitimacy and credibility, and inspire urgency and secrecy. These are used to exploit individual vulnerability in a highly personalised manner. Such interactional methods are particularly effective in exploiting the individual vulnerabilities of recipients.

Scammers use three broad techniques to distort recipients' decision-making: **addressing immediate concerns, genre-mapping and scripting.**

How scammers address the recipient's doubts

When a recipient receives a piece of mail they have to make a decision about whether to open it, and then whether to read it, or to throw it away. This early decision-making is important; the longer the exposure to and engagements with scams, the more likely the recipient will suffer a degradation in decision-making and self-control, making them more vulnerable to falling victim (Baumeister *et al.*, 2008). So the scammer aims to overcome the recipient's urge to throw the scam mail away by saying something like:

> *You don't believe it! Do whatever you want ... But read this letter anyway which is worth its weight in gold!*

Scam prevention advice often includes warnings about being pressured; however the interaction here creates the illusion that the recipient has choices ('Do whatever you want') and appears open by acknowledging the recipient will doubt the content of the letter ('You don't believe it!') rather than attempting to convince them otherwise. This openness builds trust, as by acknowledging the recipient will doubt his message, and exposing the potential for them to discard the letter, the sender shows vulnerability (Higgins and Walker, 2012; Koon and Yoong, 2013). Anticipating the recipient's doubt the use of 'you' is reassuring as it demonstrates the sender is authoritative and knowledgeable. The final 'which is worth its weight in gold' also makes the recipient more vulnerable to the scam as it is an appeal (albeit indirect) to the recipient's visceral desires (Langenderfer and Shimp, 2001).

References and testimonials are used by scammers to support their claims, and to bolster their credibility and legitimacy (Clifton and Van de Mieroop, 2010; Ross and Smith, 2011):

> *Mrs Rachel Nibbs ... Can confirm everything. In spite of all her doubts she requested the ... And became rich shortly afterwards.*

This enables the scammer to distance themselves from the message which then lends it legitimacy. Perceiving a similar experience to another builds trust and feelings of solidarity (Silvia, 2005; Stevens and Kristof, 1995), and legitimises the belief that if they act in the same way they will also receive the rewards (Jagatic *et al.*, 2007; Koon and Yoong, 2013). This reassures and encourages the recipient to suspend their disbelief and ignore these immediate concerns. The use of the phrase 'all her doubts' also suggests a range of doubts, which enables the recipient to find applicability to their own situation, which increases scam compliance (Modic and Lea, 2013).

All of these elements combine to reassure the recipient and make them vulnerable to the scam without the scammer having to use highly visible techniques such as pressurised selling.

Genre-mapping

People seek reassurance and evidence as part of the decision-making process, particularly if they are anxious (Maitlis and Ozcelik, 2004). They will focus on elements they recognise in order to decide if the communication is genuine and they can trust it. People are more likely to trust the sorts of communications that are familiar to them or which they have been exposed to previously (Zajonc, 2001). Using images and words familiar to the recipient may therefore enable scammers to exploit the bonds recipients feel towards legitimate sources of information and lead them to override rational decision-making processes that are normally based on judgement and logic. Older people are particularly vulnerable to difficulties in decision-making based on advertising (Yoon *et al.*, 2009; Shivapour *et al.*, 2002).

CASE STUDY

Genre mapping

A 'psychic' named 'Master Cosmos' wrote to recipients stating that he had been instructed to pass on an inheritance from a wealthy director of casinos in Las Vegas, named Robert. The scammer created a story about Robert embarking on an expedition.

Prior to going he told Cosmos if anything should happen to him, that an item (in essence in a chest full of riches) should be passed on to the recipient of the scam mail. Alongside the letter, there was a 'handwritten' (typed in a handwriting style typeface) letter from Robert to Cosmos on headed notepaper, explaining the situation and asking Cosmos to carry out his final wishes. The final inserts are a 'newspaper' clipping that details Robert's disappearance, and a clipping from a 'candid interview' with Cosmos.

The case study illustrates how scammers use newspapers which are familiar and often trusted sources of information; a newspaper clipping lends credibility to the story and implies the information in the scam letter can be corroborated using the multiple inserts enclosed with it. This exploits Zajonc's claims (2001) that decisions are made through feelings of familiarity, and these are then sought to be rationalised through evidence. The presence of an insert itself is also an implicit way in which the scam draws on genuine communications; inserts are widespread in magazines and newspapers, and their presence in scam mail can legitimise or lend it credibility.

The 'candid interview' with Cosmos enables him to demonstrate his legitimacy through showing that he is important and successful enough to warrant being interviewed, and that he is trusted by celebrities, e.g. 'I cannot speak about my more distinguished political or artistic consultants. Except perhaps Arnold, Sylvester and George, but they are close friends.' Celebrity endorsements increase the credibility of the message being delivered (Cugelman *et al.*, 2008). The interview clipping includes Cosmos revealing limited information about himself, but also protecting his personal life: 'I am married ... but this remains part of my Ultra Private sphere. I don't want my wife or children to be bothered by my fame ... or by your article.' This self-disclosure engenders trust in recipients, and shows his credibility (Benwell and Stokoe, 2006; Cockroft and Cockroft, 2013) through prioritising his family's privacy over his self-publicity.

By using genre-mapping, the sender shows the recipient he is fulfilling a commitment to a third party (to pass the information about the inheritance on), which compels the victim to reciprocate, drawing them into an implicit social contract (Jagatic *et al.*, 2007; Koon and Yoong, 2013). This tactic is particularly persuasive due to the altruistic and final wishes elements; it is not like typical scam tactics such as requests for money or direct orders for action (Blanton, 2012).

Scripting

Scammers use scripting to direct the recipient towards a course of action. The recipient is given a new role and identity as a winner, someone in control of their destiny, someone with good luck, the receiver of a gift, etc. and all the recipient needs to do in order to achieve it is to follow the script provided. The script narrows the decision-making options available to the recipient and makes it easier for the scammer to issue requests that would ordinarily cause alarm:

☐ *YES, Master Cosmos, please send me the wonderful* **Secret Container** *which was entrusted to you for me by our friend Robert, the Director of Gaming Casinos which makes* **hundreds of millions of pounds** *every day. What a joy to receive a Gift of Great Value and have the authorisation to open this* **Heavy Chest**.

This paragraph enables the scammer to script the victim on various levels: by ticking the box, the recipient agrees that the container exists, the situation described to them in the scam letter is real, and they believe the secret container is 'wonderful' and 'a joy to receive'. This shows the scammer scripting the recipient's description of and emotions towards the object. The script constructs the relationship the recipient has with both Cosmos and Robert. Robert is described as a mutual friend, which suggests a mutual social bond, increasing the recipient's perception of legitimacy (Jagatic *et al.*, 2007). The scammer's trustworthiness is enhanced through the mutual friend entrusting his final wishes with him. The recipient is scripted to describe the turnover of the company ('hundreds of millions of pounds every day'), although this is something the recipient would have had no knowledge of. It is in this way the sender can lead the recipient to express that the company is real, the people Master Cosmos talks of are real, and the secret container is real and about to be his.

We are anxious to receive your documentation. Please be prompt!

Here a delay is categorised as something that will cause anxiety to the sender and their associates. This shows the sender as vulnerable, which reveals their honesty (Higgins and Walker, 2012) and engenders trust (Koon and Yoong, 2013). The sender also presents a facade of credibility by showing an anxiety for the recipient through concern (Cockroft and Cockroft, 2005) that they may not respond quickly enough to receive the prize. This encourages the recipient to respond promptly, and it is important that that the sender frames their anxiety as linked to the speed of the recipient's response, rather than associated with the potential for the recipient not to respond. The absence of a question as to whether the recipient will respond removes the option of not responding from the recipient's frame of reference and implicitly delivers the message that their response is inevitable.

Summary

The three methods demonstrate a variety of communication techniques used by scammers to inform, persuade, convey credibility, demand urgency and secrecy, and provide reassurances of legitimacy. They manipulate recipients' decision-making processes, redirecting or distorting perceptions, whilst mitigating individuals' doubts or concerns.

Scam mail has the ability to appear to be directly and specifically written for the recipient, whereas in reality, identical letters will have been sent to thousands of addresses. It has transformative abilities insofar as it enables a variety of recipient concerns to be addressed; it can communicate with the recipient in a manner that is personal, familiar and reassuring to them; and it can issue instructions, directions and threats in a framework that makes them appear reasonable rather than alarming. Importantly, this enables many of the key features that are described as warning signs for potential scam mail victims (pressure to respond, calls for secrecy, requests for money) to be addressed both explicitly and in more subtle ways, through the use of 'you', self-disclosure and the removal of agency. The key elements of trust, credibility, secrecy and urgency are performed and enabled through addressing immediate concerns, genre-mapping and scripting, which are ultimately the way in which scammers manage the restrictive nature of a single speculative postal scam communication.

References

Acierno, R., Hernandez, M.A., Amstadter, A.B., Resnick, H.S., *et al.* (2010) Prevalence and correlates of emotional, physical, sexual, and financial abuse and potential neglect in the United States: The National Elder Mistreatment Study. *American Journal of Public Health*, 100: 292–7.

ACTSO (Association of Chief Trading Standards Officers) (2014) *Summary of Doorstep Crime Report to National Tasking Group*, March 2014. London: ACTSO.

ACTSO (2015) *Doorstep Crime Project Report 2014/2015*.

Adult Social Care Statistics NHS Digital (2016) *Safeguarding Adults Annual Report, England 2015–16 Experimental Statistics*. Health and Social Care Information Centre. Available from: https://www.gov.uk/government/uploads/system/uploads/attachment_data/file/557866/SAC__1516_report.pdf

Age UK (2014) *Evidence Review: Loneliness in Later Life*. London: Age UK. Available from: http://www.ageuk.org.uk/Documents/EN-GB/For-professionals/Research/Age%20UK%20Evidence%20Review%20on%20Loneliness%20July%202014.pdf?dtrk=true

Age UK (2015) *Only the Tip of the Iceberg: Fraud Against Older People*. London: Age UK. Available from: http://www.ageuk.org.uk/documents/en-gb/for-professionals/consumerissues/age%20uk%20only%20the%20tip%20of%20the%20iceberg%20april%202015.pdf?dtrk=true

Age UK (2016) *Later Life in the United Kingdom: October 2016*. London: Age UK. Available from: https://www.ageuk.org.uk/Documents/EN-GB/Factsheets/Later_Life_UK_factsheet.pdf?dtrk=true

Al-Yagon, M. and Margalit, M. (2013) Social cognition of children and adolescents with LD: Intrapersonal and interpersonal perspectives, in Harris, K., Graham, S. and Swanson, L. (eds) *Handbook of Learning Disabilities*. New York: Guilford Press, pp278–92.

Allan, K. (2001) *Communication and Consultation: Exploring Ways for Staff to Involve People with Dementia in Developing Services*. Bristol: The Policy Press.

Allpass, F., Towers, A., Stephens, C., Fitzgerald, E., Stevenson, B. and Davey, S. (2007) Independence, well-being and social participation in an aging population. *Annals of the New York Academy of Sciences*, 1114: 241–50.

Alves, L. and Wilson, S. (2008) Effect of loneliness on telemarketing fraud vulnerability amongst older adults. *Journal of Elder Abuse and Neglect*, 20 (1): 63–85.

Alzheimer's Disease International (2013) *Policy Brief for Heads of Government: The Global Impact of Dementia 2013–2050*. Available from: http://www.alz.co.uk/research/GlobalImpactDementia2013.pdf

Alzheimer's Society (2008) *Maintaining Everyday Skills*. London: Alzheimer's Society. Available from: http://www.alzheimers.org.uk/factsheet/521

Alzheimer's Society (2009) *Counting the Cost: Caring for People with Dementia on Hospital Wards*. London: Alzheimer's Society.

Alzheimer's Society (2011) *Short Changed: Protecting People with Dementia from Financial Abuse.* Available from: http://alzheimers.org.uk/site/scripts/download_info.php?fileID=1296

Alzheimer's Society (2013a) *Building Dementia-Friendly Communities: A Priority for Everyone.* London: Alzheimer's Society.

Alzheimer's Society (2013b) *This is Me Booklet.* London: Alzheimer's Society.

Alzheimer's Society (2013c) *Factsheet – Communicating 500LP.* Available from: https://www.alzheimers.org.uk/site/scripts/download_info.php?fileID=1789

Alzheimer's Society (2014) *Dementia 2014 Report Statistics.* Available from: https://www.alzheimers.org.uk/statistics

Alzheimer's Society (2016) *Demography.* Available from: https://www.alzheimers.org.uk/site/documents_info

Association of Directors of Adult Social Services, Local Government Association (2014) *Making Safeguarding Personal Guide.* Available from: https://www.adass.org.uk/media/5145/making-safeguarding-personal-guide-2014.pdf

Association of Directors of Adult Social Services, Local Government Association, NHS Clinical Commissioners and NHS Confederation (2016) *Stepping up to the Place: The Key to Successful Health and Care Integration.* Available from: http://www.nhsconfed.org/~/media/Confederation/Files/Publications/Documents/Stepping%20up%20to%20the%20place_Br1413_WEB.pdf

Bacon, N., Brophy, M., Mguni, N., Mulgan, G. and Shandro, A. (2010) *The State of Happiness: Can Public Policy Shape People's Well-Being and Resilience?* London: The Young Foundation.

Barratt, M. (2012) *Operation Liberal: Doorstep Crime Prevention, 2012 Good Practice Guide.* Ripley: Derbyshire Constabulary, Design and Print Section.

Baumeister, R.F., Sparks, E.A., Stillman, T.F. and Vohs, K.D. (2008) Free will in consumer behavior: Self-control, ego depletion, and choice. *Journal of Consumer Psychology* 18 (1): 4–13.

Benwell, B. and Stokoe, E. (2006) *Discourse and Identity.* Edinburgh: Edinburgh University Press.

Beresford, P. (2013) *Personalisation.* [Kindle edition]. Bristol. Policy Press.

Bhatia, V.K. (1993) *Analysing Genre: Language Use in Professional Settings.* New York: Longman Publishing.

Bierman, A. and Statland, D. (2010) Timing, social support, and the effects of physical limitations on psychological distress in late life. *The Journals of Gerontology Series B: Psychological Sciences and Social Sciences,* 65 (5): 631–9.

Biggs, S., Manthorpe, J., Tinker, A., Doyle, M. and Erens, B. (2009) Mistreatment of older people in the United Kingdom: Findings from the first national prevalence study. *Journal of Elder Abuse and Neglect,* 21 (1): 1–14.

Blanton, K. (2012) The rise of financial fraud: Scams never change but disguises do. *The Center for Retirement Research,* 12 (5): 1–12.

Bolton, M. (2012) *Loneliness: The State We're In: A Report of Evidence Compiled for the Campaign to End Loneliness.* Abingdon: Age UK, Oxfordshire.

Boyle, G. (2013) 'She's usually quicker than the calculator': Financial management and decision-making in couples living with dementia. *Health and Social Care in the Community,* 21 (5): 554–62.

Brammer, A. (2014) *Safeguarding Adults.* Basingstoke: Palgrave MacMillan.

Brown, H. (2003) What is financial abuse? *Journal of Adult Protection,* 5 (2): 3–10.

Button, M., McNaughton Nicholls, C., Kerr, J. and Owen, R. (2014) Online frauds: Learning from victims why they fall for these scams. *Australian and New Zealand Journal of Criminology,* 47 (3): 391–408.

Cacioppo, S., Capitanio, J.P. and Cacioppo, J.T. (2014) Toward a neurology of loneliness. *Psychological Bulletin,* 140: 1–40.

Campaign to End Loneliness (2016) *The Missing Million: A Practical Guide to Identifying and Talking about Loneliness.* Available from: http://www.campaigntoendloneliness.org/wp-content/uploads/CEL-Missing-Millions-Guide_final.pdf

Cattan, M., White, M., Bond, J. and Learmouth, A. (2005) Preventing social isolation and loneliness among older people: A systematic review of health promotion interventions. *Ageing and Society*, 25: 41–67.

Chartered Trading Standards Institute (2016) *Workforce Survey* [online]. Available from: https://www.tradingstandards.uk/media/documents/policy/strategy/ctsi-workforce-survey-2016.pdf

Chen, Y., Hicks, A. and While, A.E. (2014) Loneliness and social support of older people in China: A systematic literature review. *Health and Social Care in the Community*, 22 (2): 113–23.

Choi, N.G., Kulick, D.B. and Mayer, J. (1999) Financial exploitation of elders: Analysis of risk factors based on county adult protective services data. *Journal of Elder Abuse and Neglect*, 10 (3/4): 39–62.

Cialdini, R.B. (1984) *The Psychology and Influence of Persuasion*. New York: Quill William Morrow.

Clifton, J. and Van de Mieroop, D. (2010) 'Doing ethos': A discursive approach to the strategic deployment and negotiation of identities in meetings. *Journal of Pragmatics*, 42: 2449–61.

Cockroft, R. and Cockroft, S. (2005) *Persuading People: An Introduction to Rhetoric*, 2nd edn. London: Palgrave Macmillan.

Code of Practice for Victims of Crime (2015) https://www.gov.uk/government/uploads/system/uploads/attachment_data/file/476900/code-of-practice-for-victims-of-crime.PDF

Colley, A. (2016) Cowboy roofing scam: Elderly couple conned out of £900k. *The Bucks Free Press*, 13 July. Available from: http://www.bucksfreepress.co.uk/news/14616365.COWBOY_ROOFING_SCAM__Elderly_couple_conned_out_of___900k/

Commission for Social Care Inspection (2008) *Safeguarding Adults: A Study of the Effectiveness of Arrangements to Safeguard Adults from Abuse*. London: CSI.

Cooper, A., Briggs, M., Lawson, J., Hodson, B. and Wilson, M. (2016) *Making Safeguarding Personal Temperature Check*. Commissioned by the Association of Directors of Adult Social Services. Available from: https://www.adass.org.uk/media/5461/making-safeguarding-personal-temperature-check-2016.pdf

Cross, C. (2015) No laughing matter: Blaming the victim of online fraud. *International Review of Victimology*, 21 (2): 187–204.

Cugelman, B., Thelwall, M. and Dawes, P. (2008) Website credibility, active trust and behavioural intent, in Oinas-Kukkonen, H., Hasle, P., Harjumaa, M., Segerståhl, K. and Øhrstrøm, P. *PERSUASIVE 2008 – Persuasive Technology, Third International Conference June 4–6, 2008, Oulu, Finland*. pp47–57. Available from: http://dx.doi.org/10.1007/978-3-540-68504-3_5

Daly, L., McCarron, M., Higgins, A. and McCallion, P. (2013) 'Sustaining Place': A grounded theory of how informal carers of people with dementia manage alterations to relationships within their social worlds. *Journal of Clinical Nursing*, 22 (3–4): 501–12.

Davidson, S., Rossall, P. and Hart, S. (2015) *Financial Abuse Evidence Review*. Age UK Research. Available from: http://www.ageuk.org.uk/Documents/EN-GB/For-professionals/Research/Financial_Abuse_Evidence_Review-Nov_2015.pdf?dtrk=true

Day, T. (2015) Lost in the system: Locating rogue trading incidents in police statistics. *The International Journal of Crime Prevention and Community Safety*, 17, 189–204.

Department for Constitutional Affairs (2007) *Mental Capacity Act 2005 Code of Practice*. London: TSO.

Department of Health (DH) (2000) *No Secrets*. London: DH.

Department of Health (2003) updated 2010. *Fair Access to Care Services: Guidance on Eligibility Criteria for Adult Social Care*. London: HMSO.

Department of Health (2009) *Safeguarding Adults: Report on the Consultation of the Review of No Secrets – Guidance on Developing and Implementing Multi-agency Policies and Procedures to Protect Vulnerable Adults from Abuse*. London: TSO.

Department of Health (2013) *Statement of Government Policy on Adult Safeguarding*. Available from: https://www.gov.uk/government/uploads/system/uploads/attachment_data/file/197402/Statement_of_Gov_Policy.pdf

Department of Health (2016a) *Care and Support Statutory Guidance Issued under the Care Act 2014*. Available from: www.gov.uk/guidance/care-and-support-statutory-guidance.

Department of Health (2016b) *Prime Minister's Challenge on Dementia 2020*. London: HMSO.

Digital NHS (2016) *Personal Social Services: Expenditure and Unit Costs England 2015–16*. Available from: http://www.content.digital.nhs.uk/catalogue/PUB22240/pss-exp-eng-15-16-fin-rep.pdf

Donaldson, R. (2003) *Experiences of Older Burglary Victims* (Home Office Research, Development and Statistics Directorate, Findings No. 198). London: Home Office.

Dupré, M. (2012) Disability culture and cultural competency in social work. *Social Work Education*, 31 (2): 168–83.

Dury, R. (2014) Social isolation and loneliness in the elderly: An exploration of some of the issues. *British Journal of Community Nursing*, 19 (3): 125–8.

Eggenberger, E., Heimer, K. and Bennett, M.I. (2013) Communication skills training in dementia care: A systematic review of effectiveness, training content, and didactic methods in different care settings. *International Psychogeriatrics*, 25 (3): 345–58.

Eisend, M. (2008) Explaining the impact of scarcity appeals in advertising. *Journal of Advertising*, 37 (3): 33–40.

Europol (2011) *OC-scan threat notice 009–2011*. Available from: https://www.europol.europa.eu/sites/default/.../oc-scan-policy-brief-open-version.pdf

EWCA Crim 2545. (2012) Regina vs Tomney and others. Available from: https://www.criminallawandjustice.co.uk/clj-reporter/R-v-CS-2012-All-ER-D-06-Mar-2012-EWCA-Crim-389

Faulkner, A. and Sweeney, A. (2011) *Prevention in Adult Safeguarding: A Review of the Literature*. Social Care Institute of Excellence. Report 41. Available from: https://www.scie.org.uk/publications/reports/report41/keymessages.asp

Fenge, L. (2011) Economic well-being and ageing: The need for financial education for social workers. *Social Work Education: The International Journal*, 31 (4): 498–511.

Financial Conduct Authority (FCA) (2014) *Be a ScamSmart Investor*. Available from: http://scamsmart.fca.org.uk/page/be-a-scamsmart-investor

Financial Fraud Action (2014) *New Figures Show Steep Rise in Telephone Scams*. Available from: http://www.financialfraudaction.org.uk/cms/assets/1/phone%20scams%20press%20release%20-%20embargoed%20until%202%20dec%202014%20-%20final.pdf

Fischer, P., Lea, S. and Evans, K. (2013) Why do individuals respond to fraudulent scam communications and lose money? The psychological determinants of scam. *Journal of Applied Social Psychology*, 43 (10): 2060–72.

Flynn, M. (2007) T*he Murder of Stephen Hoskin: A Serious Case Review – Executive Summary*. Truro: Cornwall Adult Protection Committee.

Flynn, M. and Citarella, V. (2012) *Winterbourne View Hospital: A Serious Case Review*. Bristol: South Gloucester Council on Behalf of South Gloucester Safeguarding Adults Board.

Francis, R. (2013) *Report of the Mid Staffordshire NHS Foundation Trust Public Inquiry Executive Summary*. London: The Stationery Office, HC 947.

Furedi, F. (2011) *Changing Societal Attitudes and Regulatory Responses to Risk Taking in Adult Care*. York: Joseph Rowntree Foundation.

Galpin, D. (2016) *Safeguarding Adults at Risk of Harm*, 2nd edn. Bournemouth: Learn to Care.

Gibson, S.C. and Honn Qualls, S. (2012) A family systems perspective of elder financial abuse. *Journal of the American Society on Aging*, 36 (3): 26–9.

Glasby, J., Miller, R. and Needham, C. (2015) Adult social care, in Foster, L., Brunton, A., Deeming, C. and Haux, T. (eds) *In Defence of Welfare 2*. Bristol: Policy Press.

Gorden, C. and Buchanan, J. (2013) A systematic literature review of doorstep crime: Are the crime-prevention strategies more harmful than the crime? *The Howard Journal of Criminal Justice*, 52 (5): 498–515.

Gravell, C. (2012) *Loneliness and Cruelty: People with Learning Disabilities and Their Experience of Harassment, Abuse and Related Crime in the Community*. London: LemosCrane.

Hancock, M. (2016) *Government Makes it Easier to Crackdown on Nuisance Calls Crooks* [online]. Available from: https://www.gov.uk/government/news/government-Makes-it-easier-to-crackdown-on-nuisance-calls-crooks

Hawkley, L.C. and Cacioppo, J.T. (2010) Loneliness matters: A theoretical and empirical review of consequences and mechanisms. *Annals of Behavioral Medicine*, 40 (2): 218–27.

Higgins, C. and Walker, R. (2012) Egos, logos and pathos: Strategies of persuasion in social/environmental reports. *Accounting Forum*, 36: 194–208.

Higher Education for Dementia Network (HEDN) (2014) *A Curriculum for UK Dementia Education*. London: Dementia UK.

HM Government (2015) *Spending Review and Autumn Statement: Key Announcements*. Available from: https://www.gov.uk/government/topical-events/autumn-statement-and-spending-review-2015

Holtfreter, K., Reisig, M.D., Mears, D.P. and Wolfe, S.E. (2014) Financial exploitation of the elderly in a consumer context. Available from: https://www.ncjrs.gov/pdffiles1/nij/grants/245388.pdf

Holt-Lunstad, J., Smith, T.B., Baker, M., Harris, T. and Stephenson, D. (2015) Loneliness and social isolation as risk factors for mortality: A meta-analytic review. *Perspectives on Psychological Science*, 10 (2): 227–37.

Holwerda, T.J., Deeg, D., Beekman, A., Van Tilburg, T., *et al.* (2012) Feelings of loneliness, but not social isolation, predict dementia onset: Results from the Amsterdam Study of the Elderly (AMSTEL). *Journal of Neurology, Neurosurgery and Psychiatry*, 82 (2): 135–42.

Home Office (2003) *'They didn't just steal my money': Tackling Distraction Burglary. A National Distraction Burglary Taskforce Report*. London: Home Office. Available from: http://webarchive.national archives.gov.uk/20100413151441/crimereduction.homeoffice.gov.uk/burglary58.pdf

Home Office (2004) *Counting Rules for Recorded Crime: Instructions for Police Forces*. London: Home Office.

Humphries, R., Thorlby, R., Holder, H., Hall, P. and Charles, A. (2016) *Social Care for Older People Home Truths*. The Kings Fund and Nuffield Trust. Available from: https://www.kingsfund.org.uk/sites/files/kf/field/field_publication_file/Social_care_older_people_Kings_Fund_Sep_2016.pdf

Information Commissioner's Office (2015) *Data Protection Act 1998 Supervisory Powers of the Information Commissioner Monetary Penalty Notice*. Available from: https://ico.org.uk/media/action-weve-taken/mpns/1432872/helm-monetary-penalty-notice.pdf

Joiner, T.E., Lewinsohn, P.M. and Seeley, J.R. (2002) The core of loneliness: Lack of pleasurable engagement – more so than painful disconnection – predicts social impairment, depression onset, and recovery from depressive disorders among adolescents. *Journal of Personality Assessment*, 79, 472–91.

Kane, M. and Terry, G. (2015) *Dementia 2015: Aiming Higher to Transform Lives*. Alzheimer's Society. Available from: https://www.alzheimers.org.uk/site/scripts/download_info.php?downloadID=1677

Kang, Y. and Ridgway, N. (1996) The importance of consumer market interactions as a form of social support for elderly consumers. *Journal of Public Policy and Marketing*, 15 (1): 108–17.

Kich, M. (2005) A rhetorical analysis of fund-transfer-scam solicitations. *Cercles*, 14: 129–42.

Kneale, D. (2012) *Is Social Exclusion Still Important for Older People?* London: The International Longevity Centre-UK (ILC-UK).

Koon, T.H. and Yoong, D. (2013) Preying on lonely hearts: A systematic deconstruction of an internet romance scammer's online lover persona. *Journal of Modern Languages*, 23: 28–40.

Kunst-Wilson, W. and Zajonc, R. (1980) Affective discrimination of stimuli that cannot be recognized. *Science*, 207 (4430): 557–8.

Langenderfer, J. and Shimp, T.A. (2001) Consumer vulnerability to scams, swindles, and fraud: A new theory of visceral influences on persuasion. *Psychology and Marketing*, 18 (7): 763–83.

Lawson, J., Lewis, S. and Williams, C. (2014) *Making Safeguarding Personal Guide. Association of Directors of Adult Social Services and Local Government Association* [online]. Available from: http://www.local.gov.uk/documents/10180/5854661/Making+Safeguarding+Personal+-+Guide+2014/4213d016-2732-40d4-bbc0-d0d8639ef0df

Lea, S.E.G. and Webley, P. (2006) Money as tool, money as drug: The biological psychology of a strong incentive. *Behavioural Brain Sciences*, 29 (2): 161–209.

Lee, J. and Geistfeld, L. (1999) Elderly consumers' receptiveness to telemarketing fraud. *Journal of Public Policy and Marketing*, 18 (2): 208–17.

Lee, S., Johnson, R., Fenge, L. and Brown, K. (in press) Safeguarding adults at risk of financial scamming, in Cooper, A. and White, E. (eds) *Good Practice in Safeguarding Adults*. London: Jessica Kingsley.

Lindgren, B.M., Sundbaum, J., Eriksson, M. and Graneheim, U.H. (2014) Looking at the world through a frosted window: Experiences of loneliness among persons with mental ill-health. *Journal of Psychiatric and Mental Health Nursing*, 21 (2): 114–20.

Livability (2016) *Dementia Friendly Church*. Available from: http://www.livability.org.uk/blog-and-resources/training-and-events/dementia-friendly-churches/

Local Government Association (2015) *Making Safeguarding Personal Toolkit*, 4th edn. London: ADASS/LGA. Available from: http://www.local.gov.uk/documents/10180/6869714/Making+safeguarding+personal_a+toolkit+for+responses_4th+Edition+2015.pdf/1a5845c2-9dfc-4afd-abac-d0f8f32914bc

Local Government Association (2016a) *Stepping Up to the Place: The Key to Successful Health and Care Integration*. London: LGA. Available from: http://www.local.gov.uk/adult-social-care/-/journal_content/56/10180/7859151/ARTICLE

Local Government Association (2016b) *Efficiency Opportunities Through Health and Social Care Integration: Delivering More Sustainable Health and Care, Final Report*. London: LGA. Available from: http://www.local.gov.uk/documents/10180/11553/Productivity+and+commissioning+-+LGA+Efficiency+opportunities+through+integration+FINAL-WEB.pdf/5c920eb6-a86e-43d9-96dc-f6fab7015846

Local Government Association (2016c) *Combating Loneliness: A Guide for Local Authorities*. London: LGA.

Local Government Association and Association of Directors of Adult Social Services (2014) *Making Safeguarding Personal 2013–14: Report of Findings*. London: LGA.

Local Government Association and Ernst and Young (2015) *Creating a Better Care System*. Available from: http://www.local.gov.uk/publications-list/-/journal_content/56/10180/7350693/PUBLICATION

Lonsdale, J., Schweppenstedde, D., Strang, L., Stepanek, M. and Stewart, K. (2016) *National Trading Standards: Scams Team Review*. Cambridge: The RAND Corporation. Available from: http://www.rand.org/pubs/research_reports/RR1510.htm

Lubben, J., Gironda, M., Sabbath, E., Kong, J. and Johnson, C. (2015) *Social Isolation Presents a Grand Challenge for Social Work*. American Academy of Social Work and Social Welfare Working Paper No. 7. Available from: http://aaswsw.org/wp-content/uploads/2015/03/Social-Isolation-3.24.15.pdf

Luo, Y., Hawkley L.C., Waite, L.J. and Cacioppo, J.T. (2012) Loneliness, health, and mortality in old age: A national longitudinal study. *Social Science and Medicine*, 74: 907–14.

Lymbery, M. (2013) Reconciling radicalism, relationship and role: Priorities for social work with adults in England. *Critical and Radical Social Work*, 1 (2): 201–15.

McEvoy, P. *et al.* (2014) Dementia communication using empathic curiosity. *Nursing Times*, 110 (24): 12–15.

McEvoy, P. and Plant, R. (2014) Dementia care: Using empathic curiosity to establish the common ground that is necessary for meaningful communication. *Journal of Psychiatric and Mental Health Nursing*, 21 (6): 477–82.

Maitlis, S. and Ozcelik, H. (2004) Toxic decision processes. *Organization Science*, 15 (4): 375–93.

Manthorpe, J., Stevens, M., Rapaport, J., Harris, J., *et al.* (2009) Safeguarding and system change: Early perceptions of the implications for adult protection services of the English individual budgets pilots – A qualitative study. *British Journal of Social Work*, 39 (8): 1465–80.

Margalit, M. (2012) *Lonely Children and Adolescents: Self Perceptions, Social Exclusion and Hope.* New York: Springer.

Marson, D.C., Martin, R.C., Wadley, V., Griffith, H.R., *et al.* (2009) Clinical interview assessment of financial capacity in older adults with mild cognitive impairment and Alzheimer's disease. *Journal of the American Geriatrics Society*, 57 (5): 806–14.

Melchiorre, M.G., Chiatti, C., Lamura, G., Torres-Gonzales, F., *et al.* (2013) Social support, socio-economic status, health and abuse among older people in seven European countries. *PloS one*, 8 (1): p.e54856.

Ministry of Justice (2008) *Mental Capacity Act 2005: Deprivation of Liberty Safeguards Code of Practice to supplement the main Mental Capacity Act 2005 Code of Practice.* London: TSO.

Mitchell, L., Burton, E. and Raman, S. (2004) Dementia-friendly cities: Designing intelligible neighbourhoods for life. *Journal of Urban Design*, 9 (1): 89–101.

Modic, D. and Lea, S.E.G. (2013) *Scam Compliance and the Psychology of Persuasion. Social Science Research Network.* Available from: http://dx.doi.org/10.2139/ssrn.2364464

National Council of Aging (2015) *10 Top Scams Targeting Seniors.* Available from: https://www.ncoa.org/economic-security/money-management/scams-security/top-10-scams-targeting-seniors/

National Fraud Authority (2013) *Annual Fraud Indicator.* Available from: https://www.gov.uk/government/uploads/system/uploads/attachment_data/file/206552/nfa-annual-fraud-indicator-2013.pdf

National Trading Standards (2016) *Protecting Consumers and Safeguarding Businesses.* Available from: http://www.nationaltradingstandards.uk/

National Trading Standards Board, National Tasking Group (2015) *Doorstep Crime Project Report 2014/15.* National Trading Standards Board, North Yorkshire.

National Trading Standards Scams Team (2015) *Scams Toolkit: A Holistic Guide to Mail Fraud.* Available from: http://www.nationaltradingstandards.uk/search/?q=Scams+Toolkit%3A+A+Holistic+Guide+to+Mail+Fraud

Nicholl, A. (2014) *Neighbourhood Approaches to Loneliness: A Briefing for Local Government.* York: Joseph Rowntree Foundation.

Office of Fair Trading (OFT) (2006) Research on Impact of Mass Marketed Scams: A Summary of Research into the Impact of Scams on UK Consumers (No. OFT 883). Available from: http://www.icfs.org.uk/~icfs.org.uk/images/pdfs/60.pdf

Office of Fair Trading (2009) *The Psychology of Scams: Provoking and Committing Errors of Judgement.* London [online]. Available from: https://ore.exeter.ac.uk/repository/handle/10871/20958

Office for National Statistics (2015) *Measuring National Wellbeing: Insights into Loneliness, Older People and Wellbeing.* Available from: https://webcache.googleusercontent.com/search?q=cache:dx91KcUIStsJ:https://www.ons.gov.uk/peoplepopulationandcommunity/wellbeing/articles/measuringnationalwellbeing/2015-10-01/pdf+&cd=3&hl=en&ct=clnk&gl=uk

Office for National Statistics (2017) *Statistical Bulletin: Crime in England and Wales: Year Ending September 2016.* Available from: https://www.ons.gov.uk/peoplepopulationandcommunity/crimeandjustice/bulletins/crimeinenglandandwales/yearendingsept2016

Office of the Public Guardian (2007) *Mental Capacity Act 2005: Code of Practice.* London: The Stationery Office.

O'Keeffe, M., Hills, A., Doyle, M., McCreadie, C., *et al.* (2007) *UK Study of the Abuse and Neglect of Older People.* NatCen/ King's College London. Available from: http://www.natcen.ac.uk/media/308684/p2512-uk-elder-abuse-final-for-circulation.pdf

Olivier, S., Burls, T., Fenge, L. and Brown, K. (2015) 'Winning and losing': Vulnerability to mass marketing fraud. *Journal of Adult Protection,* 17 (6): 360–70.

Operation Liberal (2014) *Annual Report 2013–2014.* Unpublished internal document.

Operation Liberal (n.d.) *Health and Social Care Doorstep Crime Prevention Training Manual.* Nottingham: Operation Liberal Publishing.

Oxford English Dictionary (2017) Available from: www.oed.com

Penninx, B.W., Van Tilburg, T., Kriegsman, D.M., *et al.* (1999) Social network, social support, and loneliness in older persons with different chronic diseases. *Journal of Aging Health,* 11: 151–68.

Penny, J. (2015) *Public Services and (In)equality in an Age of Austerity.* New Economic Foundation and The British Council. Available from: www.britishcouncil.org

Peplau, L.A. and Perlman, D. (eds) (1982) *Loneliness: A Sourcebook of Current Theory, Research and Therapy.* New York: Wiley.

Phillips, C. (2016) *Doorstep Crime: Prisoner Interviews.* Report for National Trading Standards Doorstep Crime Project, June 2016.

Prince, M., Knapp M., *et al.* (2014) *Dementia UK: Update.* London: Alzheimer's Society.

Projecting Older People Population Information (POPPI) (2015) *Living Alone.* Available from: http://www.poppi.org.uk/ (registration required for free access to the document).

Rabiner, D.J., O'Keeffe, J. and Brown, D. (2005) A conceptual framework of financial exploitation of older persons. *Journal of Elder Abuse and Neglect,* 16 (2): 53–73.

Redmond, M. (2016) From 'intrusive' and 'excessive' to financially abusive? Charitable and religious fund-raising amongst vulnerable older people. *Journal of Adult Protection,* 18 (2): 86–95.

Research in Practice for Adults (Updated 2016) *Working with People Who Self-Neglect: Practice Tool.* Available from: https:// www.ripfa.org.uk/resources/publications/practice-tools-and-guides/working-with-people-who-selfneglect-practice-tool-updated-2016

Richman, S.B., Pond Jr, R.S., Dewall, C.N., Kumashiro, M., Slotter, E.B. and Luchies, L.B. (2016) An unclear self leads to poor mental health: Self-concept confusion mediates the association of loneliness with depression. *Journal of Social and Clinical Psychology,* 35 (7): 525–50.

Romeo, L. (2015) Making adult safeguarding personal. *Journal of Adult Protection,* 17 (3): 195–204.

Ross, S. and Smith, R.G. (2011) *Risk Factors for Advance Fee Fraud Victimization – Trends and Issues in Crime and Criminal Justice 420.* Australian Government: Australian Institute of Criminology.

Ruck-Keen, A., Butler-Cole, V., Allen, N., Bicarregui, A., Kohn, N. and Akhtar, S. (2016a) *A Brief Guide to Carrying Out Capacity Assessments.* 39 Essex Chambers. Available from: http://www.39essex.com/content/wp-content/uploads/2016/08/ Capacity-Assessments-Guide-August-2016.pdf

Ruck-Keen, A., Butler-Cole, V., Allen, N., Lee, A., Bicarregui, A. and Edwards, S. (2016b) *A Brief Guide to Carrying Out Best Interests Assessments.* 39 Essex Chambers. Available from: http://www.39essex.com/content/wp-content/uploads/2016/08/ Best-Interests-Assessments-Guide-August-2016.pdf

Ryan, E.B., Meredith, S.D., MacLean, M.J. and Orange, J.B. (1995) Changing the way we talk with elders: Promoting health using the communication enhancement model. *International Journal of Aging and Human Development,* 41 (2): 89–107.

Ryser, L. and Halseth, G. (2011) Informal support networks of low-income senior women living alone: Evidence from Fort St. John, BC. *Journal of Women and Aging*, 23: 185–202.

Samsi, K., Manthorpe, J. and Chandaria, K. (2014) Risks of financial abuse of older people with dementia: Findings from a survey of UK voluntary sector dementia community services staff. *Journal of Adult Protection*, 16 (3): 180–92.

Santini, Z.I., Fiori, K.L., Feeney, J., Tyrovolas, S., Haro, J.M. and Koyanagi, A. (2016) Social relationships, loneliness, and mental health among older men and women in Ireland: A prospective community-based study. *Journal of Affective Disorders*, 204: 59–69.

Scambusters (2014) Available from: http://www.scambusters.com

Sherraden, M., Laux, S. and Kaufman, C. (2007) Financial education for social workers. *Journal of Community Practice*, 15 (3): 9–36.

Shevlin, M., McElroy, E. and Murphy, J. (2014) Loneliness mediates the relationship between childhood trauma and adult psychopathology: Evidence from the adult psychiatric morbidity survey. *Social Psychiatry and Psychiatric Epidemiology*, 50: 591–601.

Shivapour, S., Nguyen, C., Cole, C. and Denburg, N. (2002) Effects of age, sex, and neuropsychological performance on financial decision-making. *Frontiers in Decision Neuroscience*, 6 (82): 1–15.

Silvester, K. (2016) Skeleton Staff. TS Review. *The Trading Standards Journal*. August, 7: 20–3.

Silvia, P.J. (2005) Deflecting reactance: The role of similarity in increasing compliance and reducing resistance. *Basic and Applied Social Psychology*, 27 (3): 277–84.

Smith, B. (2010) Treatment of dementia through cultural arts. *Care Management Journals*, 11 (1): 42–7.

Social Care Institute of Excellence (SCIE) (2011a) *Assessment: Financial crime against vulnerable adults*. Report 49 [online]. Available from: https://www.scie.org.uk/publications/reports/report49.asp

Social Care Institute of Excellence (SCIE) (2011b) *Black and Minority Ethnic People with Dementia and Their Access to Support and Services, Research Briefing 35*. London: Social Care Institute for Excellence.

Social Care Institute for Excellence (SCIE) (2012) *People not Processes: The Future of Personalisation and Independent Living*. London: Social Care Institute for Excellence. Available from: http: www.scie.org.uk/publications/reports/report55/

Social Care Institute of Excellence (SCIE) (2013) *Dementia Gateway: Knowing the Person Behind the Dementia*. Available from: http://www.scie.org.uk/dementia/resources/files/knowing-the-person-behind-the-dementia.pdf

Social Care Institute for Excellence (SCIE) (2014) *Care Act 2014. Context of the Mental Capacity Act 2005 (MCA) in Gaining Access to an Adult Suspected of Being at Risk of Neglect or Abuse: A Guide for Social Workers and Their Managers in England*. Available from: http://www.scie.org.uk/care-act-2014/safeguarding-adults/adult-suspected-at-risk-of-neglect-abuse/law/mca2005.asp

Social Care Institute for Excellence (SCIE) (2015a) *Preventing Loneliness and Social Isolation Among Older People*. Available from: http://www.scie.org.uk/publications/ataglance/ataglance60.asp

Social Care Institute for Excellence (SCIE) (2015b) *Adult Safeguarding Practice Questions*. Available from: https://www.scie.org.uk/search?sq=+Adult+safeguarding+practice+questions

Social Care Institute for Excellence (SCIE) (2016) *Role and Duties of Safeguarding Adults Boards*. Available from: https://www.scie.org.uk/care-act-2014/safeguarding-adults/safeguarding-adults-boards-checklist-and-resources/role-and-duties.asp

Sofaer, M. (2012) *Can the Court Protect Vulnerable Adults who have Capacity?* Available from: http://www.familylawweek.co.uk/site.aspx?i=ed101172

Sprangers, S., Dijkstra, K. and Romijn-Luijten, A. (2015) Communication skills training in a nursing home: Effects of a brief intervention on residents and nursing aides. *Clinical Interventions in Aging*, 10: 311.

Steele, B., Thornton, A., McKillop, C. and Dover, H. (2001) *The Formulation of a Strategy to Prevent and Detect Distraction Burglary Offences Against Older People (Police Award Scheme)*. London: Home Office.

Stevens, C.K. and Kristof, A.L. (1995) Making the right impression: A field study of applicant impression management during job interviews. *Journal of Applied Psychology*, 80 (5): 587–606.

Stiegel, L.A. (2012) An overview of elder financial exploitation. *Generations*, 36 (2): 73–80.

Swaffer, K. (2014) Dementia: Stigma, language, and dementia-friendly. *Dementia*, 13 (6): 709–16.

Tan, J. and MacMillan, J. (2004) The discrepancy between the legal definition of capacity and the British Medical Association's guidelines. *Journal of Medical Ethics*, 30: 427–9. Available from: http://jme.bmj.com/content/30/5/427.full

Taylor, M.G. and Lynch, S.M. (2004) Trajectories of impairment, social support, and depressive symptoms in later life. *Journal of Gerontology: Social Sciences*, 59 (4): S238–46.

The College of Social Work (2014) *National Skills Academy and Skills for Care, 2014. Care Act Learning and Development Materials* [online]. Available from: www.skillsforcare.org.uk/Documents/Standards-legislation/Care-Act/Guide-to-the-Care-Act-2014-learning-and-development-programme.pdf

Think Jessica (2015) Available from: http://www.thinkjessica.com

Think Local Act Personal (2016) *Care and Support Jargon Buster* [online]. Available from: http://www.thinklocalactpersonal.org.uk/Browse/Informationandadvice/CareandSupportJargonBuster/

Thomas, J. and Evans, J. (2010) There's more to life than GDP but how can we measure it? *Office of National Statistics. Economic and Labour Market Review*, 4 (9): 29–36.

Thompson, J., Kilbane, J. and Sanderson, H. (2008) *Person Centred Practice for Professionals*. Milton Keynes: Open University Press.

Thornton, A., Hatton, C. and McGraw, C. (2006) *Nurse for Victims of Distraction Burglary: An Evaluation of the London Borough of Islington Crime and Disorder Partnership*. London: Islington Council.

UK Trading Standards (2016) *What Do Trading Standards Do?* Available from: http://uktradingstandards.co.uk/what-do-trading-standards-do/

University of Portsmouth Counter Fraud Studies (2016) *Annual Fraud Indicator 2016*. Available from: http://www.port.ac.uk/media/contacts-and-departments/icjs/ccfs/Annual-Fraud-Indicator-2016.pdf

US Department of the Treasury (2016) *Treasury Sanctions Individuals and Entities as Members of the Pacnet Group*. Available from: https://www.treasury.gov/press-center/press-releases/Pages/jl5055.aspx

US Immigration and Enforcement Agency (2010) *Mass Marketing Fraud: A Threat Assessment*. International Mass-Marketing Fraud Working Group June 2010. Available from: https://www.ice.gov/doclib/cornerstone/pdf/immfta.pdf

Vaizey, E. (2015) *Government cracks down on nuisance calling companies*. HM Government. Available from: https://www.gov.uk/government/news/government-cracks-down-on-nuisance-calling-companies

Van Gorp, B. and Vercruyesse, T. (2012) Frames and counter-frames giving meaning to dementia: A framing analysis of media content. *Social Science and Medicine*, 74, 1274–81.

Which? (2016a) *How to Stop Nuisance Phone Calls*. Available from: http://www.which.co.uk/consumer-rights/advice/how-to-stop-nuisance-phone-calls

Which? (2016b) *Consumer Protection from Unfair Trading Regulations 2008*. Available from: http://www.which.co.uk/consumer-rights/regulation/consumer-protection-from-unfair-trading-regulations-2008

Whitty, M. (2013) The scammers persuasive techniques model: Development of a stage model to explain the online dating romance scam. *British Journal of Criminology*, 53 (4): 665–84.

Whitty, M.T. and Buchanan, T. (2012a) *The Psychology of the Online Dating Romance Scam*. Leicester: University of Leicester.

Whitty, M.T. and Buchanan, T. (2012b) The online dating romance scam: A serious crime. *Cyber Psychology, Behavior, and Social Networking*, 15 (3): 181–3.

Wild, K., Wiles, J.L. and Allen, R.E. (2013) Resilience: Thoughts on the value of the concept for critical gerontology. *Ageing and Society*, 33 (1): 137–58.

World Health Organization (WHO) (2007) *Global Age-Friendly Cities: A Guide.* Geneva: WHO Press. Available from: http://www.who.int/ageing/age_friendly_cities_guide/en/

World Health Organization (2008) *A Global Response to Elder Abuse and Neglect: Building Primary Health Care Capacity to Deal with the Problem Worldwide: Main Report.* Available from: http://www.who.int/ageing/publications/ELDER_DocAugust08.pdf

World Health Organization (2012) *Dementia: A Public Health Priority.* Geneva: WHO Press.

World Health Organization (2016) *Dementia: Fact Sheet.* Available from: http://www.who.int/mediacentre/factsheets/fs362/en/

Wright, T. (2014) Reconceptualising dementia-friendly communities. *Diversity and Equality in Health and Care*, 11 (3/4): 282–3.

Yoon, C., Cole, C.A. and Lee, M. (2009) Consumer decision making and aging: Current knowledge and future directions. *Journal of Consumer Psychology*, 19 (2): 1610–16.

Zajonc, R.B. (2001) Mere exposure: A gateway to the subliminal. *Current Directions in Psychological Science*, 10 (6): 224–8.

Zeiling, H. (2013) Dementia as a cultural metaphor. *The Gerontologist*, 54 (2): 258–67.

Case law

Aintree University NHS Hospitals Trust v James [2014] UKSC 67

A Local Authority v DL [2010] EWHC 2675 (Fam): [2011] EWHC 1022 (Fam): [2012] EWCA Civ 253

HL v UK [2004] 40 EHRR 761

Kings College NHS Foundation Trust v C and V [2015] EWCOP 80

P (by his litigation friend the Official Solicitor) v Cheshire West and Chester Council and another: P & Q (by their litigation friend the Official Solicitor) v Surrey County Council [2014] UKSC 19

PC & NC v City of York Council [2013] EWCA Civ 478

R v Tomney [2012] EWCA Crim 2545

R v Turnbull [1976]

The PCT v P, AH and the Local Authority [2009] EW Misc 10 (COP)

Legislation

Human Rights Act 1998

Youth Justice and Criminal Evidence Act 1999

Proceeds of Crime Act 2002

Mental Capacity Act 2005

Fraud Act 2006

MCA Code of Practice 2007

The Consumer Protection from Unfair Trading Regulations 2008

Equality Act 2010

Care Act 2014

Index